The Path
Trusting God and Loving People

CLAIRE MOYE

WESTBOW
PRESS®
A DIVISION OF THOMAS NELSON
& ZONDERVAN

WestBow Press books may be ordered through booksellers or by contacting:

WestBow Press
A Division of Thomas Nelson & Zondervan
1663 Liberty Drive
Bloomington, IN 47403
www.westbowpress.com
1 (866) 928-1240

Unless otherwise indicated, all Scripture quotations are taken from the Holy Bible, New Living Translation, copyright © 1996, 2004, 2007 by Tyndale House Foundation. Used by permission of Tyndale House Publishers, Inc., Carol Stream, Illinois 60188. All rights reserved.

ISBN: 978-1-9736-0650-5 (sc)
ISBN: 978-1-9736-0651-2 (e)

Library of Congress Control Number: 2017915377

Print information available on the last page.

WestBow Press rev. date: 12/29/2017

This book is dedicated to Jason Moye, without whom I would never have woken up, realized I was wandering, and found The Path.

Contents

Foreword

Unfortunately, Christians have a reputation to face. We can be some of the most hurtful and judgmental people in America, all in the pursuit of trusting God and loving people! We think we are doing the right thing, the godly thing, when in reality many of us are either stomping on our brothers, or we're burned out people-pleasers who allow ourselves to be used or abused in the name of Jesus.

I wrote this study because I resembled both of those descriptions at one point or another. I didn't understand that my past experiences combined with my assumptions about the Christian life were interfering with how I trusted God and loved people. But thank God, my eyes were opened and I learned how to examine what I actually believed about myself, God, and other people to find what was causing carnage in my relationships – including my relationship with God (though I thought it was great!).

This study is designed to help you examine the beliefs and preconceived assumptions you have about your Christian life (that you don't even know are there) so that you can trust God and love people without wounding them, or yourself, in the process.

GROUP STUDY

This study is designed as a group study. Sharing our lives with others is where the grace of God is put into practice. We gain strength and hope when we realize we are not struggling alone in this messed up world. Hearing other people's stories helps us learn about ourselves. If you are doing this study on your own, you will need a friend you can trust to bounce your thoughts off of; preferably someone who won't try to fix you or tell you what to do, but who will allow you to wrestle with yourself through this process. Often, we lose our perspective when we keep things to ourselves. We need the perspective of someone outside of our own mind to keep our own perspectives in check.

STARTING A GROUP

If you are starting a group, please see the **Group Leaders Guide** at the end of this workbook.

The Path

Introduction

Imagine this:

A man wakes up in the woods. He has no idea where he is. As he looks at his surroundings he notices a map and a compass on the ground next to him. Curious, he opens the map and inspects it, finding an X with "Camp" written underneath. He eventually realizes that he must use the compass and map to help him find the camp.

He picks up the compass and finds north, then looks at the map. Since he doesn't know if he's north, south, east, or west of the camp, just looking at his compass won't help him. If he assumes he knows where he is and chooses a direction based on that assumption it's highly unlikely he'll magically choose the one that leads directly to the camp.

He then inspects the map. The camp is located in a crescent shaped valley near a stream. When he scans his surroundings he sees nothing but trees and some craggy rocks. How is he going to use the map to help him find his way if he can't see the stream or the valley? He could head out in search of those landmarks, but that could take forever, especially if he is several miles or ridgelines from that area.

What piece of information does this man need in order to find the right path to his camp? He needs to find out his *own location* on the map. He must examine the area around him and explore the terrain until he finds similarities on the map that can indicate where he is. Only then can he use the map and compass to take the path that will lead him to the camp.

You may be asking what in the world this analogy has to do with you. The same concept is true in your Christian life. Many of us got saved and headed off to do the will of God without looking at our location. That is:

> *our preconceived thoughts and beliefs about ourselves, others, circumstances, and God that have developed over our lives thus far and that have been shaped by our experiences.*

There's really not a word that encompasses all of that so we'll just call it our "stuff".

The church in general spends a lot of time (much like the Pharisees) explaining the do's and don'ts of the path – love God, follow Jesus, love others, forgive, pray, do good, avoid sin, don't drink, smoke, or chew, or go with girls who do, etc. ;-) Rarely do churches emphasize the importance of examining our stuff so that we don't end up hurting people when we interpret God's will through our stuff-colored glasses. I think it's safe to say that most churches don't even know how to teach us how to examine our stuff – our location – shaped by our unique past. In fact, many of us were told that we *shouldn't* focus on ourselves. That's completely backward! "Judge not lest you be judged" and "get the plank out of your own eye" means we must examine ourselves—not to focus on ourselves selfishly, but to make sure we're submitting all of our stuff. Too many of us just have no idea where we are. We've never even considered it.

If we don't know where we are, what happens when we take off to follow God's commands? What does that look like in real life? Let's look at the command to love others. Some of us have developed low self-worth from our past experiences. Maybe we have come to believe that everything that goes wrong is our fault. That's our current location. When we try to follow the command to love others without dealing with those beliefs it's very likely we will let others walk over us or abuse our efforts to be loving. We confuse love with people-pleasing, or we become a martyr. Our beliefs in that area shape the way we interpret and carry out the command to love.

Maybe the opposite is true and we have pride in our lives. We may have gotten the idea that a good Christian always has an answer for everyone about everything. In that case it's likely we will follow that same command to love others by spewing out advice when they mention their problems, or trying to control them and change them. We confuse love with interference. (And just so you know, that's my personal experience. More on that later.) Our preconceived beliefs determine the path we take and we end up hurting ourselves and others.

It's not enough to ask, "Am I loving others?" and stop there. My interpretation of love might be way off as the examples above illustrate. We must delve deeper. We must ask, "How am I carrying out the command to love others?" "Am I trying to control?" "Am I letting myself be used or abused?" "Why do I think that's love?" "What does God say about how to love?" Etc.

Adam and Eve were the first sinners. They only committed one sin (or maybe 3 or 4 depending on how detailed you want to get). Their eyes were opened and they knew they had sinned, knew they were naked, and they hid from God. What was the first question God asked them? "Where are you?" Did He ask because he didn't know? Of course not! He could have zapped the bushes and revealed their location, shouting, "Found you, you prideful, untrusting, greedy sinners!" But He didn't. Once they came out of hiding, God asked, "Who told you that you were naked? Have you eaten of the tree of which I commanded you not to eat?" Again, was God unaware of what they had done? Of course He knew! Then why did He ask the questions? I believe it was because He had a personal relationship with Adam and Eve and He wanted them to openly admit their disobedience – for *their* good, not God's.

We are new creations, right? "The old has gone… the new has come." God is all-powerful, the Holy Spirit guides us, Jesus paid for our sin and we have His righteousness. The Bible is the Living Word and is capable of revealing truth to us. Yes. Absolutely. No disagreement there. Our old selves were dead in our sins but our spirits have been born again, made new in God's kingdom. But does God just teleport us to camp the minute we accept Jesus as our savior? Does Jesus erase our past and make us behave perfectly at the moment of salvation? I wish that were true. Wouldn't that be great? I know some people have had issues like anger, for example, disappear when Christ entered their lives. I believe that God does that at times. However, if Jesus made us all perfect and erased our past and its effects on us at the moment of salvation then why are there so many problems in the Christian community?

Shouldn't we ALL be like huge magnets to the unsaved like Jesus was, not driving them away? Shouldn't we ALL be able to get along amongst ourselves? Shouldn't hypocrisy, divorce, greed, addictions, selfishness, and prideful attitudes be nonexistent in our congregations? Why are those and countless other problems still here? Can you imagine a world where all Christians always do what Jesus would do and give mercy and love like He did? Why isn't that happening now? Let's get more personal. Why don't you always act like Jesus? Why don't you carry out God's will perfectly? It's obvious we each have our own stuff causing us to walk around in circles in the woods. Why is it that we either hide, or refuse to look at our location just like Adam and Eve?

God can make everything in our lives perfect in an instant, but He doesn't. Salvation is 100% on Him. There's nothing we can do to save ourselves. Once we accept His salvation, however, He wants our submission, and that requires *action* on our part. He wants us to examine our location, our stuff, because He wants us to admit where we are and willingly hand our stuff over to Him. Adam could have said, "Hey, God! Naked? No! We just had this great idea for these awesome new loincloths! Aren't they fashionable?" How would that have affected his relationship with God?

James 2:17 says, "Faith that doesn't show itself by good deeds is no faith at all – it is dead and useless." Similarly, when we refuse to examine our real deep-down stuff or refuse to admit specific sins, we are ultimately not trusting that Jesus' death on the cross is sufficient to change and heal us. Our belief is useless and dead. It's not that God can't heal us in an area we just won't look at, it's that our denial breaks our relationship with Him. Our obstinacy keeps us from actively submitting to Him. Our refusal to even consider that we might be on our own path indicates that we don't trust that God will forgive us, open His arms, and say, "That's ok. I love you! Walk with Me this way instead."

On the other hand, there are those of us who see our sins all too well. We have no problem admitting that we're messed up but we don't know what to do with all our stuff. We don't know how to find our location, so to speak. All we see are the trees and rocks in our way. We try to clean up our lives over and over again but never seem to succeed. It seems like Jesus won't take it away. Why is that, especially when we want to be rid of it with all our hearts? Could there be something in our stuff that's causing us to hang on to it? There probably is, and we won't be able to loosen our grip on our stuff until we know what it is. Then we can submit it to God and start down the path to camp.

This may not be the perfect analogy. A map and compass in the woods cannot adequately represent our relationship with the Almighty Trinity and the Bible. Pretty much any analogy in this imperfect world would break down at some point if carried far enough. I believe this analogy does help explain the amount of hurt and hypocrisy present in the church, that is to say, Christians (which means you and me) today. So stay with the basic idea as we go on and don't get hung up on it being exact.

Looking at our stuff is not about condemning ourselves, but experiencing freedom! It may *seem* condemning because we're not proud of our stuff and we don't want it to be there. Just because you don't look at the huge boulder chained to your leg doesn't mean you won't be crippled by it. Just because you don't realize there's a huge magnet in your pocket doesn't mean your compass will read true north. You will live with your stuff every day and it will affect every relationship in your life if you don't acknowledge it and submit it to God. That is when you will find true freedom in Christ. His death on the cross means you don't have to be ashamed, no matter what kind of stuff you find! Nothing negates the power of the cross! Your stuff is exactly why Jesus went to that cross! So take courage! There is NO condemnation for those who are in Christ Jesus!

In this study we will learn to examine our lives in order to find any stuff that is damaging our relationships or keeping us from trusting God (our location). When we find that stuff, we submit it to God, trust Him, and make things right in our relationships (the path). Then we share our struggles and victories with others and continue to examine our lives until we reach complete maturity (camp) on that day when Christ Jesus comes back again.

> "And I am sure that God, who began the good work within you, will continue his work until it is finally finished on that day when Christ Jesus comes back again." (Phil 1:6)

The Path

The purpose of this study is to find our location (the stuff that is damaging our relationships and keeping us from trusting God) so we can follow the path (trusting God and loving others) until we reach camp (complete maturity) on the day Jesus returns. This is what that looks like:

Humility - Waking Up in the Woods

I realize that there are areas of my life I have tried to navigate on my own and that not knowing my location has gotten me lost.

Trust - Believing that Only God Can Lead Me to Camp

I make sure I really believe that God's way is better than mine (because I see mine has gotten me lost), and trust that He will guide me onto the right path when I surrender my stuff to Him.

Honesty - Finding my Location

I take an honest, and fearless (because I trust God) look at my stuff – my preconceived thoughts and beliefs about myself, others, circumstances, and God that have developed over my life thus far and that have been shaped by my experiences – which is keeping me off the right path.

Restoration - Walking the Path

Part I - Restore my relationship with God by admitting my stuff, submitting each piece to Him, and allowing Him to lead me (because I found areas where I was off the path).

Part II - Restore my relationships with others by making amends with people I've hurt and forgiving those who've hurt me (because this is God's path).

Fellowship - Helping Others Wake Up

I share my experience with others both for their encouragement and my humility (because someone else's sharing helped me wake up in the woods).

Maturity - Checking my Direction

I evaluate my thoughts and actions on a daily basis for the rest of my life to make sure I'm still following God to camp and not doing things my own way (because ignoring my location was what got me lost in the first place).

Group Guidelines

This group is different from a typical Bible Study where everyone shares their thoughts on the Bible. Because it is focused on wrestling with the personal struggles going on in each of our own lives, respecting what other people share is vital. This is what that looks like:

Focus on your own thoughts and behavior, not on blaming others or on what other people have shared. Do not give advice to anyone or correct anything anyone shares. It doesn't matter if they're way off in your theological opinion - they need to share freely in order to figure out their own stuff. Let them. If you're unsure about the scriptural truth of something shared, look it up yourself or ask your pastor. Don't interrupt anyone; let them finish their thoughts, even if they're stumbling through them. Don't talk with your neighbor while someone is sharing. Also, don't hog sharing time; keep it to a few minutes so that everyone has a chance. Above all else, do not talk about what anyone shares outside of this group. Respecting confidentiality is essential for honesty. If you break confidence you may be asked to leave the group because it will be harder for people to be open and honest around you.

*Group leaders: there is a more detailed explanation of the reason for these guidelines in the group leader's guide at the back of this workbook.

Humility

Waking Up in the Woods

*I realize that there are areas of my life I have tried to navigate on my
own and that not knowing my location has gotten me lost.*

First things first. Before we can find our location, we need to wake up. Look around. Humility means seeing yourself exactly where you are in relation to God and others. As far as God goes, He knows stuff I don't. He can see the future. He can heal cancer. He can make donkeys talk (look that one up!). He can change a person's mind and heart. I can't do any of that stuff! I don't even know what's best for myself half the time (although I think I do, but then look what a mess I make!), let alone the entire world. When I do things my way, I make things worse. I don't know the answers to everything, but God does and I'll submit myself to Him and let Him lead my life. That's humility in relation to God. He is perfect; I cannot hope to take His place. Not in my own life, or in anyone else's.

As far as others go, we're all in the same woods – this life. Not one of us can even attempt to reach complete maturity on our own. The Bible says all our attempts to be good are like filthy rags (Isa. 64:6). That literally translates to used menstrual cloths. If you cringed when you read that like I did writing it, that's the reaction we're going for. Let that sink in. We are all the same in that respect. That's extremely critical to grasp. The righteousness we have because of Jesus is *His* righteousness, *not ours*, so we don't get to take any credit for it. Not one of us is better than anyone else. In fact, if you think you're better than someone else, you're actually proving you're not (hint: pride). Humility in relation to others means I believe I'm no better or worse than anyone else. I might not have done the same things or been through the same problems, but without Jesus, I'm just as lost. Honestly, I have a tendency to wander off the path just like everyone else.

If you believe you are already on the right path, at least pause and take another look to make sure you're still on course. After all, Satan is always throwing obstacles in our way. Let's say you got your bearings and headed out in the right direction. What happens if you never check your compass, map, and location again? You will run into a cliff or a stream (problem relationships, unforeseen circumstances, selfish thoughts, etc.) that you have to navigate around and you'll end up off course. Even dodging trees and rocks will nudge you off course little by little. So, where are you lost in the woods? What path are you taking in your own wisdom? Let's take a quick look around.

> First, take a moment and ask God to reveal some stuff to you as we continue. That is, ask Him to reveal the people you might not be treating with humility and love (including yourself), and places where you're trying to cram life into the odd-shaped box you've created.

Next, consider these areas:

Your relationships: Do you get along with everyone all the time? Which people irritate you? Are there certain people you constantly argue with? Do people always do what you want them to do? If not, is that frustrating? If so, are those relationships loving and joyful? How do others respond to you? Are there people who treat you poorly? Who are abusive? Are you too hard on yourself, or too easy? Take thirty seconds to write down some difficult relationships (use code names if you need to!).

_____

_____

_____ .

Your circumstances: Do they always go your way? If not, is that okay? Is it maddening? Or just a disappointment? Can you control what happens to you? What happens when you try? Do you resent a person or incident that negatively affected your life? Do problems keep coming up that you ignore or consider someone else's problem? Do you avoid certain places or things because of a bad experience? Do you think some circumstances will never change? What has happened in the past, or is happening to you right now, that did not, or is not going the way you want it to? Quickly jot down the first things that come to mind.

_____

_____

_____ .

Your responsibilities: Are you getting everything on your plate done? If so, are you exhausted? Is everything you've put on your plate really your responsibility? If not, are you trying to earn something or control someone? Are you allowing others to take over your responsibilities? Why? Are you short-changing yourself? Are you lazy? Does any of the above frustrate you? Write down a few quick examples.

_____

_____

_____ .

Now, how are you handling these people and things? Most of us fall into one of two categories:

1) Some of us try to handle difficulties and frustrations by controlling them. We think it's our job to tell everyone where they're messing up. We think we can change people and situations and we begin trying to force them to be and do what we think is right. We scold and punish or flatter and manipulate. We criticize other people's behavior, especially if we think it reflects badly on us. But we justify our own behavior, either because we think that we're right or because we're just reacting

to someone or something else. In fact, the more we focus on correcting and controlling others' stuff the less we focus on controlling our own. Of course then our own lives get out of control because we're ignoring our stuff. And the more out of control our lives get the more we try to fix it by controlling others. What a vicious cycle!

2) Some of us handle difficulties and frustrations by checking out. We figure we can't change a person or situation so why bother doing anything? It may show up as passive irresponsibility, like getting that paycheck but doing just enough to not get fired. Or going out to the garage when an argument is brewing. Or having so much to do that you hardly ever see a particular person or you don't have time to get to that certain chore. Avoid, avoid, avoid.

Or we may go into active irresponsibility, responding to a difficult situation by showing just how destructive we can be. It's the "I'll show them!" mentality. (S)he thinks you spend too much - you go on a shopping spree. A loved one dies suddenly or leaves you and now you're pushing everyone away so you won't get hurt again. You suffer abuse only to turn around and abuse someone else. You've been hurt in any one of several ways and you turn to alcohol, drugs, food, gambling, etc. to numb the pain. Destroying your own life to get back at someone else.

> Group Discussion: Which of these describes you? Is it working? Is it helping you love God and others? Share your thoughts.

Either way, it all really boils down to selfish control – trying to control life, either overtly or covertly, on our own with our own wisdom, in our own strength, with our own justifications, Biblically based as they may be. That, my friends, is the opposite of Humility. That is pride. Even if you feel like the lowest of the low, anything you try to accomplish on your own is a rejection of the cross. We handle things on our own without knowing it because of our stuff – our preconceived thoughts and beliefs about ourselves, others, circumstances, and God that have developed over our lives thus far and that have been shaped by our experiences. If we haven't examined our stuff we are doomed to keep wandering in the woods, reacting in hurtful and unhelpful ways.

I fall into the first category. I was raised in a Christian home – a really good one! Somehow I learned that I had to have all the answers. I thought I had to give the Holy Spirit's advice to other people. With my friends I was a mild advice giver (I think!), but when I got married, Katie, bar the door! My husband had to believe the same things, react the same way, and like the same things as I did. I critiqued him all the time. I felt that his behavior was a reflection on me. Now, he's Latino and I'm English. Emotionally he's fiery and we joke that I'm a robot. He's an introvert and I'm an extrovert. How do you think changing him into me worked out?

I was playing God! I was making my husband my god and demanding he meet my needs my way! I was controlling and shaming and doing it all in the name of Jesus! Just remembering that time makes me cringe! I didn't know my stuff. I didn't know I even needed to examine it. I didn't know it was there because I'd had such a "good" Christian life. I was following Jesus, and praying, and asking for guidance, but here's the catch – I was doing that focusing on changing my husband

and giving good advice to others. I was not praying as King David did, "Search me, Oh God, and know my heart; test me and know my thoughts. Point out anything in me that offends you, and lead me along the path of everlasting life." (Psalm 139:23-24 NLT)

Thankfully, one day I woke up. I looked at my surroundings, squinting and blinking, and was dumbfounded! Here I thought I was on the right path, but really I had no idea where I was. I had taken off to find camp with no idea what my own location was and I was hurting other people and myself instead of loving and encouraging them God's way. I was causing my own problems because I couldn't get out of the way and let God do His job. That day I realized that I was the chief among sinners. I went from being the Pharisee at the wall praying, "Thank you God that I'm not a sinner like everyone else." To being the tax collector praying, "Oh God, be merciful to me, for I am a sinner." (see Luke 18:9-14)

That was the day I was humbled and admitted I was living my life my way, not God's. That was the day I began to surrender my stuff and heal. That was the day I truly began to trust God! Not myself!

I have not "arrived" at camp by any means, nor will I until the day I die or Jesus returns. I still wander off the path on an almost daily basis because my ideas of how to live life clash with others' ideas – because we're just different. I think God intentionally made us different from one another so we could learn to be unselfish. Our default path is selfishness. It takes intention to be unselfish. That's why it's so important to look around. I don't ever mean to hurt anybody, but I do it unintentionally all the time. If I ignore that, it's like hiding in the bushes with a fig leaf. It hurts my relationship with God and with other people.

Your life may be like mine, or it may be the complete opposite. It does not matter! We all have stuff! We need to stop blaming other people for our controlling, avoiding, or destructive behavior. We need Humility. We need to stop focusing on where other people or institutions are falling short. We need to start looking at the sin – yes, sin – behind our stuff. We'll do that in more detail later. For now, just get to the place where you are willing to look around and admit you are relying on yourself in *some* area. Look back at the people, circumstances, and responsibilities you wrote down at the beginning of this chapter. Can you see *one* area you've handled on your own and made a mess of? If you can't, pray David's prayer. Chances are you're hiding.

The truth is that Jesus has already freed us from sin, but it is also true that we don't always act like it. There are two types of people in this world: those who can be honest about where they wander off the path, and those who can't. If you can be honest about where you are you will find healing and freedom. Those are the people who truly trust that God loves them and can heal them. If you can't be honest with yourself and God about where you are, don't expect anything in your life to get better. Not because God can't handle it or Jesus' death doesn't cover it (it does!), but because you won't unclench your fist to surrender it. Deep down, you don't trust God with your mistakes.

Whether you're off the path one degree, or 180 degrees the result is the same. You miss camp. You miss the maturity that comes with letting go of your own will, trusting God, and loving people His way. One degree takes you way off course after a hundred miles, and this is a lifelong journey with obstacles all along the way. Once you can be humble and admit you're off the path wandering in the woods, you can begin to trust God to lead you.

Group Discussion: Read Job 38:1 – 42:5 as a group. Share your thoughts on humility.

LOCATION CHECK

You may read through and discuss these suggestions, questions, and verses as a group, but they are meant for you to work through in detail on your own. You don't have to do every suggestion, answer every question, or read every verse. Just focus on the ones that speak to you. There is room at the end of this chapter to write your thoughts if you wish.

SUGGESTIONS

Fold a piece of paper in half lengthwise. On the top of one column write <u>Mine</u> and on the other side write <u>Not Mine</u>. In the Mine column write all the areas of your life that are your responsibility – from chores to attitudes. Note if you have a good handle on them, or if they're being ignored or managed poorly. For instance, you can control you children's bedtime, but not whether they go to sleep. In the Not Mine column write down all the areas of your life that you can't control or that are not your responsibility. You can't control anyone's salvation, for instance. Use the questions below if you need help. Pray that God will give you insight, honesty, and courage.

QUESTIONS

The following questions are designed to help jumpstart your thinking.

- Do I generally see myself as better than others? Do I generally see myself as worse than others? Why?
- Do I realize and accept that I cannot control another person's behavior? How have I tried to control others? What was the outcome?
- Do I understand that God created other people with different strengths, weaknesses, and preferences from me? That they also have their own stuff to deal with?
- Am I able to ask for help or do I have to have all the answers? Why?
- What have I done to get what I want and need? Have I forced, manipulated, argued, etc.?
- When others refuse to do what I want, how do I respond? Why?
- What do I think would happen if I stopped trying to change others? How can I stop?
- When am I embarrassed or ashamed because of someone else's behavior?
- Do I seek approval and acceptance from others? How does that affect my life?
- Am I actively seeking my location or am I following the path I think is right? Am I taking responsibility for examining my own stuff? How? Why?
- How do I handle the smooth times? Do I constantly look for problems? Why?
- Am I restless when I am alone? Do I feel comfortable being alone with myself?
- Do I agree that God is able to speak to others apart from my influence?

RELATED SCRIPTURE

Look up the following verses. What do they say about doing things our own way?

2 Kings 5:9-15

Luke 15:13-17

Romans 7:18-20

Romans 12:16

1 Corinthians 3:18-20

1 Corinthians 4:1-7

1 Corinthians 8:1-2

A few more verses on this subject:
Genesis 16:1-15, Exodus 18:13-18, Judges16:20, Job 38:1 – 42:5, Ecclesiastes 5:1-2, Matthew 7:3-5, Matt 23: 2-8, Luke 6:37, John 15:4-5, Romans 9:31-32, Romans 14:1-23, 2 Corinthians 4:7, Philippians 2:3-7

Thoughts

Thoughts

Trust

Believing that Only God can Lead me to Camp

I make sure I really believe that God's way is better than mine (because I see mine has gotten me lost) and trust that He will guide me onto the right path when I surrender to Him.

Now we know we're lost in the woods. It's dawned on us that we have some stuff to deal with. We see that we've strayed off the path at some point. What do we do? If we panic and start to correct our course by getting rid of our stuff on our own, were just doing the same thing that got us lost in the first place. That's called insanity. Remember that we thought we were on the right path to begin with. Correcting our course ourselves is futile. "There is a path before each person that seems right, but it ends in death" (Prov. 14:12). That meaning doesn't have to be limited to our salvation. That can refer to relationships, finances, sexuality, responsibility, you name it! We must stop going down the path that seems right, submit our stuff, and allow Jesus to lead us to His path.

In John 14:23 Jesus says, "All those who love me will do what I say." Loving God = obeying God. 1 John 5:3 says, "Loving God means keeping his commandments, and really, that isn't difficult. For every child of God defeats this evil world by trusting Christ to give the victory." Are we going to obey someone we don't trust? No! So to me, loving God = trusting God. I like how Jim Burgen from Flatirons Community Church puts it in many of his messages: "Believe that Jesus is who He says He is, will do what He says He will do, and will keep every promise He's ever made to you." That, in a nutshell, is Trust. (Just a quick reminder here; Jesus does not promise us a trouble-free life.)

I know we as Christians say we trust God, but so many times our thoughts and actions betray that. We tend not to trust God to handle other people in our lives, especially our family members, but also bosses, fellow church members, and dare I say politicians! Before you say, "Of course I don't trust them," look back at the beginning of the sentence. It says we tend not to trust *God*, not other people! Remember, other people stray off the path just like we do. We are not asked to put our total trust in people. Our spouse hurts us, intentionally or not, because we're just different. We snap at the kids because we're upset about something else. Or more damaging, someone has abused us, cheated us, or abandoned us. I'm not saying we should swing to the other extreme and refuse to trust anyone. What I am saying is that no matter *what* happens, we can put our absolute trust in God. That means we can trust Him with other people.

When we don't trust God with other people some of us tend to start telling them what they should do. Paul says, "Who are you to condemn God's servants? They are responsible to the Lord, so let Him tell them whether they are right or wrong. The Lord's power will help them do as they should" (Romans 14:4). Did you know this verse was in the Bible? I didn't. I found this verse after I woke up to my controlling behavior. I realized that I was not trusting God, I was playing God. I thought that if I didn't speak up, the other person would never know what they were doing wrong and how to fix it. How arrogant of me! God is the only one who is capable of changing a person's heart.

They might not even need correction. It might be MY stuff that's causing the problem – especially if I haven't looked at it.

Think about the people you've tried to correct, give advice to, or fix. How'd they take your "helpful" suggestions? Probably not well. Do you know that when you attempt to fix someone, you actually step in front of God? You block their view of God. The Lord is helping them do as they should. He's working in their lives, even though you might not see it (after all, He works on the inside). When you step in and take over, you and your well meant but hurtful, judgmental words become the target of their resentment. Whatever issue you confronted disappears behind your unwelcome correction. If the other person starts justifying the problem (assuming it's their problem and not really yours) you just caused them to harden their heart in that area. Stop trying to control and fix! Get out of the way and let God work. Just be an encouragement to them. It will be much more effective, I guarantee. Trust God to work in His way and His timing.

There is a time to help (not fix) someone else who is wandering, but we can't do that effectively until we've dealt with our own stuff and are on the path ourselves. In Jesus' words, until we've taken the plank out of our own eye (Matt 7:3-5). If we've never looked at our stuff and don't know where we are then we have a long way to go before we can help without hurting others or ourselves. Figure out your own location first, then you can help others find theirs.

> Group Discussion: What relationships are you trying to manipulate and control? Family? Friends? Boss? Church members? Where does that come from?

Instead of controlling others, some of us show our distrust of God by letting others walk all over us. We may have been told or treated like we're stupid, worthless, or a nuisance. We may have been constantly criticized or ignored. That creates some pretty hurtful stuff. Because of that stuff we're too busy trying to please others or avoid anger, abuse, and disappointment to ask God what He wants for us. When you're trying to gain approval and acceptance from people, you aren't free to be the incredible person God wants you to be. He made you unique for a specific purpose. If you're afraid of disapproval from people, following God's path for you will be impossible.

Trusting God means we get our worth from Him. He accepts us, fully and completely. He wants our lives to ultimately glorify Him. He will give us the power to do anything He asks us to do. God's power works best in our weakness. Why is that? Because it puts His strength on display. We can't possibly match the strength and power of God, so we don't even have to try. God does not help those who help themselves. He helps us do what we could never do for ourselves. Instead of constantly trying to please others, we say no to other people when He wants us to, we stand up to follow God instead of our critics, and we trust that He will defend us from those who criticize and condemn.

> Group Discussion: Do you have a tendency to get run over by others? Do you have a negative view of yourself that hinders your trust in God? Where does that come from?

We also have a tendency not to trust God with circumstances. A real eye-opener for me was when we moved thinking our house was sold. When the sale fell through I freaked out a little – ok, a lot! I became anxious, watching and waiting for another phone call from our realtor telling me the good news that our house had sold again. One day that phone call came and I was so relieved! The pressure was finally off...until *that* sale fell through. I freaked out again and tried to find any way we could salvage the sale, like my force of will could make it happen. We couldn't keep up our mortgage and our rent payments forever! It finally sold a year after we moved, and the day after closing I remember thinking that if I had only known it would all work out I wouldn't have been so anxious.

Bam! It was like a mental forehead slap when I realized that *God* knew it would all work out! He knew it all, so I didn't have to know. I could have trusted Him. I should have trusted Him! Then I realized that - wow - I didn't trust God with my life the way I thought I did. I was off the path. Thankfully, God loves me and helped me see where I was so I could get back on the path and trust Him. Years later when the same situation happened again, you can bet I remembered to trust God. What a difference that experience was! He took care of us and my trust in Him was strengthened. I'd like to think that if we still owned that house today, I would still trust that my God can handle it. That's a much better way to live.

> Group Discussion: What circumstances have you struggled with on your own? Job loss? Health problems? Financial setbacks? Natural disasters? Repossession? Something else? What are you doing to try to fix it?

In the last chapter we focused on the fact that we're all off the path somewhere. No one is any better than anyone else at navigating life on our own. You are no worse than anyone else, either, even though that message may be at the core of your stuff. Trusting God means we believe He loves and accepts us despite our mistakes and regardless of what others tell us or how they treat us. Romans 5 tells us that while we were trying to find the path on our own, weak and wandering in circles in the woods, Christ died for us and saved us because He loved us so much.

When God created the world He knew everything that was going to happen. He knew everything you would do and think. Everything! He made you and died for you anyway! It was His plan A, not plan Oops-I-didn't-see-that-coming. Think about it; nothing about us surprises God. He knows all, is everywhere, and is all-powerful. That means you can trust Him with everything. Jesus says His yoke is easy and His burden is light (Matt 11:29-30). That's not because believing and trusting in Him makes life easy, it's because when life gets hard we can trust Him to work it for good, whether we see it or not. We stop wandering in circles of controlling, manipulating, worrying, avoiding, and hiding. We ask God for guidance and we follow it, trusting Him for the results, not our own efforts.

> Group Discussion: Where do you struggle to trust God? Which people do you have trouble trusting God with? Where have you laid down your own will and trusted God?

There's a paradox here. Our righteousness is like menstrual cloths. None of us can measure up to God. None of us is better than anyone else. Yet God loves us with an unconditional and everlasting love! We are worth so much to Him that He would go through the torture of the cross for us! We cannot be righteous on our own but God sees all the righteousness of Jesus when He looks at us. Even while you were still sinning, turning your back on God and doing things your own way, Jesus died a humiliating, agonizing death for you. Knowing that makes it easier to look at your stuff and find your location. After all, He knew where you would be when he died for you and he knows where you are now. He really can stand to look at your stuff. Once you can grasp that, you can stand to look at it, too.

We must look at it, or we aren't being honest with ourselves or God.

LOCATION CHECK

You may read through and discuss these suggestions, questions, and verses as a group, but they are meant for you to work through in detail on your own. You don't have to do every suggestion, answer every question, or read every verse. Just focus on the ones that speak to you. There is room at the end of this chapter to write your thoughts if you wish.

SUGGESTIONS

Write down your view of God and how you arrived at that concept. Think about your thoughts and actions – do they line up with what you say you believe? Does your true belief line up with who God says He is in the Bible?

Choose one area where you have a hard time trusting God, but are willing to give it a try. Write it down and every morning tell Him (and yourself) you trust Him with it ask Him to take care of it. Decide what action you will take if you find your mind dwelling on it or you start taking care of it yourself. Thank God every night for His help and trustworthiness. "Giving thanks is a sacrifice that truly honors me," says the Lord. (Psalm 50:23)

QUESTIONS

The following questions are designed to help jumpstart your thinking.

- Do I really trust God with every area of my life? How can I know?
- Have I experienced God's guidance and faithfulness in my life? How?
- When I think about trusting God with a specific issue, how does that make me feel?
- What consequences have I experienced from trying to handle things my way?
- Can I trust in God's goodness and love even when circumstances look bad? Am I experiencing this now?
- Where am I stepping in front of God in someone else's life?
- How do I know what God wants me to do in a given situation?
- Am I doing anything on my own? In my own wisdom and power? What?
- How can I just follow God's leading and let go of the results?
- What can I do when other people make decisions I don't like?
- How can I let others find God's will for their own lives as I am finding mine?
- Have I allowed others to take the place of God in my life? How?
- Has my thinking become distorted by trying to please others instead of God? How?
- What am I going to do if _____ (person, place, thing) doesn't come through?
- Do I trust God to change and heal me? If not, why? If so, how does that affect my thoughts and actions?

RELATED SCRIPTURE

Look at the following verses. What do they have to say about trusting God?

Deuteronomy 30:19-20

Psalm 118:6-9

Isaiah 40:28-31

Mark 9:23-24

Romans 8:38-39

2 Corinthians 1:8-10

1 John 5:1-5

A few more verses on this subject:
Exodus 3:10 – 4:17, Psalm 34:18-22, Psalm 119: 45, Psalm 139:13-18, Psalm 145:8-21, Proverbs 3:5-8, Jeremiah 29:11-13, Matthew 11:28-30, Matthew 14:22-33, Matthew 26:39, Mark 4:35-40, Mark 10:27, John 14:12-14, 2 Corinthians 3:5, Philippians 2:13, 1 Peter 5:6-7

Thoughts

Thoughts

Honesty

Finding My Location

I take an honest and fearless (because I trust God) look at my stuff (my preconceived thoughts and beliefs about myself, others, circumstances, and God that have developed over my life thus far and that have been shaped by my experiences) which is keeping me off the path.

First of all, let me address those of us who still question the necessity of looking at our stuff and finding our location. After all, Jesus paid it all, right? To look at ourselves for flaws in thinking, mistakes in behavior, or unconscious habits means we're denying Jesus' cleansing power and not living in our new identity as a new creation. Maybe we think that we're opening ourselves up to Satan's attacks by being willing to look at our past and shortcomings. May I suggest that the exact opposite is true?

Jesus did die for all our sins. Our stuff is covered by His blood and sacrifice. It has no power over us…*but what WE give it.* And, my friend, hiding, denying, and refusing to search out and submit our stuff gives it power! To refuse to look at our preconceived thoughts and beliefs about ourselves, others, circumstances, and God that have developed over our lives thus far and that have been shaped by our experiences, is to turn our backs on the sacrifice of Jesus. We deny that the cross is powerful enough to overcome them. We keep them chained to our ankle for lack of submitting them to Jesus. It's like trying to find the path on our own with our eyes shut.

> "This is the message He has given us to announce to you: God is light and there is no darkness in Him at all. So we are lying if we say we have fellowship with God but go on living in spiritual darkness. We are not living in the truth. But if we are living in the light of God's presence, just as Christ is, then we have fellowship with each other, and the blood of Jesus, His Son, cleanses us from every sin. If we say we have no sin, we are only fooling ourselves and refusing to accept the truth. But if we confess our sins to Him, He is faithful and just to forgive us and to cleanse us from every wrong. If we claim we have not sinned, we are calling God a liar and showing that His word has no place in our hearts" (1 John 1:5-10).

Are you willing to bring your whole self into the light? John says above that we have the choice to live in the light of God's presence, or to live in spiritual darkness. To live in the truth and be cleansed from every sin or to call God a liar. You *are* forgiven and cleansed, but you won't live that way if you're holding on to sin. We need to experience the freedom that true repentance brings. Not a repentance of Adam's sin, the generic sin that is so easy to admit to, "Yes, I'm a sinner saved by grace," but a repentance of your specific, deep-down, embarrassing stuff that is hard to admit for fear of what others will think of you. That stuff that keeps us from the fellowship of God and each other—that keeps us off the path and wandering in the woods.

Whether you've been a Christian for fifty years or five minutes you have hurts, bad habits, and misconceptions that determine how you act and react. You may have trust issues, legalistic beliefs, walls of protection, guilt for something you've done wrong, or for something you haven't done. You may think that you are responsible for everything, or nothing. You may be controlling, blaming, judging, dismissive, or vindictive. You may feel worthless, inadequate, envious, fearful, or just plain indifferent. Self-centered or self-pitying? Domineering or withdrawn? Worrisome? Lazy? Resentful? Impatient? Do you even know what you are really like deep down? If you don't, chances are it's oozing out everywhere and affecting all your relationships without your knowledge.

One note of caution: if you are not living in humility and do not trust God you will not be able to take an honest look at your stuff. You will either justify it or get so defeated that you will bury yourself under it and add more on top. If you find yourself resentful at the very suggestion of examining yourself, or if the idea overwhelms you with guilt and self-condemnation, *please go back to chapter one and start over.* There is no condemnation in Christ Jesus, and, as you read above, justifying yourself is calling God a liar. If you cannot be absolutely honest with yourself, and if you don't Trust God with every part of you, you will not be able to find your location and submit your stuff. If you decide to go on and take a look, do not be afraid! God is with you! He promises to forgive and heal when we confess, but we can't confess what we won't acknowledge.

> Group Discussion: Where do you come down on the idea of examining your stuff?
> Are you overwhelmed, suspicious, indignant, intrigued? Share your thoughts with
> the group or with a trusted friend. Give grace to those who are struggling with
> this concept.

So how do we do this honest examination thing?

We come with an attitude of humility, we trust God and ask Him to guide us, and we take an honest look at our stuff using one of several models included in the LOCATION CHECK section that helps us to be objective. In the book *The Eight Points of the Oxford Group*, C. Irving Benson writes, "Repentance requires a recognition of the facts about ourselves...The capacity of the human mind for self-deception is unlimited. The Cross enables us to be sincere with ourselves – it is the one place in life where we cannot play the hypocrite".[1] That's what we're doing when we decide to get honest. We sit down with God and look at the facts about ourselves, free from judgement and condemnation. We find out where we are.

This is not about our identity. If you put your trust in Jesus as your savior you are a child of God and nothing will change that. Nothing. In Neil Anderson's book *Victory over the Darkness*, he calls us "a saint who occasionally sins."[2] When we examine ourselves it is important to know who we are in Christ and all the positive attributes Christ gives us. What we believe about ourselves does affect how we act. The list of who we are in Christ from Neil's book is included at the beginning of the LOCATION CHECK section for encouragement. Study it – it's the truth! That does not mean, however, that we should ignore the areas where we "sin occasionally." Many of us are willing to tolerate a certain level of dysfunction in our lives without doing anything about it, but Jesus has called us to live differently! It's precisely *because* of who we are that we need to examine what we do.

It may seem like a daunting task, especially if you don't have any idea how to set started. In the LOCATION CHECK section there are several ways to start the process. No one way will work for everyone but the goal of each is the same, to try to get to the bottom of our beliefs and actions so we can make sure they're based in God's truth. If you find one method isn't working, change to another. It will be helpful over the course of your life to do this several times. As we uncover and submit items in our pile of stuff new ones will be uncovered. Sometimes our lives change in unexpected ways and we become lost in the woods again. As we continue to navigate this life, it is always a good idea to examine our motives, beliefs, and actions and surrender them to God.

Each method works in a similar way. First, you need to have some means of writing everything down. Whether that's a notebook, computer, or some other device, use whatever works best for you. Next, pray. You need the revelation and protection of God as you examine your life. Then you will write about your life in different ways depending on the method. After that, you will look back and determine your part – what you did and believed, how you reacted and contributed, and where you have issues and resentments. Finally, you will look at the root cause of your part in each case. Root causes are things like fear, selfishness, pride, lack of trust in God, vengeance, feelings of worthlessness or entitlement, etc. You may need to study what the Bible has to say on a subject before you can determine your part or a root cause. If you're having trouble seeing clearly you could talk through things with a friend who demonstrates this level of honesty in their own lives (choose wisely!). Once you have determined the root cause you will know your location! You'll know why you ended up off the path. You can then start walking the path of restoration with God and other people detailed in the next chapter.

Examining yourself is going to take some time and determination. After all, you are a wonderful and complex individual, with your own unique past, character, and relationship with God. If you're overwhelmed, I suggest setting aside a specific amount of time to start with (maybe only thirty minutes if you're really overwhelmed) and just begin thinking and writing. When the time is up, stop and schedule the next time. Little by little you will make progress. Others may want to set aside a whole day or weekend to finish the entire thing at once. The important part is just to start. It could take two months or two years depending on how much time you devote to the task. That's ok! Progress, not perfection. Just keep plugging away. You'll be making discoveries and submitting your life to God all along the way, and that will help you to heal and start walking the path.

LOCATION CHECK

You may read through and discuss these suggestions, questions, and verses as a group, but they are meant for you to work through in detail on your own. You don't have to do every suggestion, answer every question, or read every verse. Just focus on the ones that speak to you. There is room at the end of this chapter to write your thoughts if you wish.

SUGGESTIONS

First, examine who you are in Christ. In Neil Anderson's book *Victory Over the Darkness*, he lists some things the Bible says are true about us once we commit our lives to Jesus:

I Am Accepted in Christ

I am God's child (John 1:12). I am Christ's friend (John 15:16). I have been justified (Romans 5:1). I am united with the Lord and one with Him in spirit (1 Corinthians 6:17). I have been bought with a price; I belong to God (1 Corinthians 6:20). I am a member of Christ's body (1 Corinthians 12:27). I am a saint (Ephesians 1:1). I have direct access to God through the Holy Spirit (Ephesians 2:18). I have been redeemed and forgiven of all my sins (Colossians 1:14). I am complete in Christ (Colossians 2:20).

I am Secure in Christ

I am free forever from condemnation (Romans 8:1). I am assured that all things work together for good (Romans 8:28). I am free from any condemning charges against me (Romans 8:33, 34). I cannot be separated from the love of God (Romans 8:35). I have been established, anointed and sealed by God (2 Corinthians 1:21). I am hidden with Christ in God (Colossians 3:3). I am confident that the good work God has begun in me will be perfected (Philippians 1:6). I am a citizen of heaven (Philippians 3:20). I have not been given a spirit of fear, but of power, love, and a sound mind (2 Timothy 1:7). I can find grace and mercy in time of need (Hebrews 4:16). I am born of God and the evil one cannot touch me (1 John 5:18).

I Am Significant in Christ

I am the salt and light of the earth (Matthew 5:13, 14). I am a branch of the true vine, a channel of His life (John 15:1, 5). I have been chosen and appointed to bear fruit (John 15:16). I am a personal witness of Christ's (Acts 1:8). I am God's temple (1 Corinthians 3:16). I am a minister of reconciliation (2 Corinthians 5:17-20). I am God's coworker (2 Corinthians 6:1). I am seated with Christ in the heavenly realm (Ephesians 2:6). I am God's workmanship (Ephesians 3:12). I may approach God with freedom and confidence (Ephesians 3:12). I can do all things through Christ who strengthens me (Philippians 4:13). [3]

You may want to look back at these for encouragement as you dig into your life.

Next, start to examine your stuff. There are several ways to do this listed below. You may choose any way that feels comfortable to you, or use a combination of methods. You will learn what to do with all this in the next chapter, but for now, just figure out your location - where you are on the map. Do this as unemotionally as you can and with lots of grace. You'll never see the path if all you do is cry or kick rocks in anger at being lost. At some point you must settle down and look around. There is no need to berate yourself for where you are today. Just ask God to guide you, take a breath, and look around. Eventually you will find that you're getting somewhere!

———— • ————

One method is to take several sheets of paper and write headings like "resentments," "anger," "sex," "pride," "dishonesty," etc.… on each one. Looking at the character checklist at the end of this section might help you find areas you struggle with. Write all you can about issues in your life for each area. When you are finished look at each area and write down what you are responsible for in each incident. Asking yourself the 4 Cs is a great way to do this.

Cause, Control, Cure, Contribute. [4]
Did I Cause the problem? If so, how?
Can I Control it? How have I tried?
Do I have the power to Cure (fix) it? How have I tried?
Did my behavior Contribute to the problem? How?

No matter what someone else's behavior was, focus on what you did that was wrong or how your behavior developed negatively as a result. You are not responsible for another person's behavior. You can, however, look at how that has affected your behavior and thinking. Your problem may be a circumstance, not a person. What do you believe about yourself and life that caused you to react the way you did? Are expectations, habits, and negative thinking causing problems in your relationships today? What are they? Then go back and try to determine the *root cause* of your behavior or thinking. Were you insecure? Why? Afraid? Why? Self-righteous? Why? Try to determine why you don't trust God in that area. Continue this process as each new issue comes to your attention over the next weeks, months, and years.

———— • ————

You may choose to dedicate an entire notebook to examine your stuff, dividing each issue into sections like this:

1. "Name" - Write the name of a person, place, or issue you struggle with.

    Example: My husband

2. "The Cause" - Write what happened that caused the hurt, fear, or problem. Be as specific as you can. You may want to leave some space after this in case you remember more to add at a later date.

> *Example:* He argues with me all the time. Every time I want to go out and do something he gets mad at me and we end up in a fight.

3. "The Effect" - Write down how that action affected your past and how it is affecting your present. Look at the area of your life on which it has had an impact. Has it affected your relationships, your sense of security, your pride, your sexuality? In this section you will begin to see trends in your behavior as you look at how your sinful behavior developed based on how you handled problems in your life.

> *Example:* I'm mad. I feel alone. I feel like I'm putting my life on hold. I don't feel like he likes me or thinks I'm attractive which makes me want to get out of the house more and be with other people.

4. "My Part" – Look at and write down what part of the conflict you are responsible for. What is the *root cause* of your action or reaction? Fear? Pride? Selfishness? Something else? You must look at your responsibility apart from what others may have done. Someone else's sinful behavior is not a reason for you to sin in return.

> *Example:* Why doesn't he want to do things with me? He hates everything I want to do. What does *he* want to do? Have I ever asked him? He has a stressful job, maybe he doesn't want to go to a loud concert with lots of people. I haven't asked him what he wants to do (selfish). I have argued with him about going out and made him feel like what I want to do is more important than him (pride). I've started to value others' company over his. (Borderline unfaithfulness – basically selfishness)

That's a very simple example, but hopefully you get the idea. Keep going until every issue of every relationship you can think of has been examined in this way. There may only be a few at first, but as you continue to ask God to reveal things to you there will be more over time.

———◦———

You can write a life story, putting the important events in your life into a narrative. For example, "I grew up in a family where my mother was _____ and my father was _____. When I was five I remember_____. It made me feel _____ and I started _____ because of it." Etc. When you are finished, you will look back over it and write down your part and the root cause (fear, anger, selfishness, lust, etc.) of your responses or actions in the margin.

———◦———

The Character Checklist included at the end of this chapter can help you break down your general character into specific thoughts and behaviors. You can complete one checklist for your character in general, or you can choose to complete one checklist for each of your problem relationships. You may find that you react differently to your spouse, boss, co-worker, or neighbor based on the nature of your relationship with them. When you have completed the checklist write down the *root cause* of your negative behavior in each instance. You can also use the checklist to help you think about what your part is in all the other methods.

As you go through examining your stuff you may have a suspicion that you are dealing with problems with alcohol, drugs, sex, co-dependency, or overeating, among others. Programs specific to those issues have something called "inventories" that help in this area. You can order a workbook from most of those programs by looking up "fourth step inventory" on Amazon.

Or, you may start by answering the questions below.

QUESTIONS

The following questions are designed to help jumpstart your thinking.

- Am I ready to take an honest look at myself? Why or why not?
- Have I sought the help of God and a trusted friend?
- What do "honest" and "fearless" mean to me?
- What does "examine my stuff" really mean?

POSITIVE CHARACTERISTICS

- How am I:
  o Caring? Am I kind to others? To myself?
  o Trustworthy?
  o Honest? Do I tell the whole truth? If not, why not?
  o Respectful? To people? To things? To the law?
  o Generous?
  o Open with others?
  o Practical?
  o Dependable? Do I do what I say I will do?
  o Responsible? Do I do what needs to be done when it needs to be done?
  o Optimistic?
  o Humble? Do I ask God for guidance? Do I ask others for help? Do I admit my mistakes?

- Where am I talented?
- Am I able to make friends easily? Why or why not?
- Am I able to see the humor in life? Am I able to laugh at myself?
- How do I practice my trust in God? Am I grateful for God's provision in my life?
- Do I trust God in dealing with others? Do I remove myself from potentially dangerous situations?
- Do I listen to the group and accept that others have needs different from mine?
- In what ways do I take care of myself?
- Do I look for the good in others?
- Am I respectful and open to another person's point of view?

NEGATIVE CHARACTERISTICS

- How am I:
  - Dishonest? Do I practice what I preach? Do I lie to save my pride? Have I hidden mistakes from others?
  - Fearful? Do I have any fears? What do I fear? Why?
  - Selfish? Do I insist on my way? Why?
  - Judgmental? Do I constantly criticize others? Do I hurt others with truth? Why?
  - Irresponsible? Do I do what I say I will do? Do I let other people take over my responsibilities? Why?
  - Self-pitying? Am I always complaining? Do I have a "woe-is-me" attitude?
  - Resentful? Do I harbor grudges? Why?
    - Do I resent anyone from the past? Why? What was my part?
    - Do I resent anyone in my immediate environment? Why? What is my part?
    - Do I resent people in authority? Why? What is my part?
    - Do I resent any places or things? Why? What is my part?
    - When do I judge others decisions or actions and then resent them for not doing what I think they should?
- Do I expect others to always do what I deem to be the right thing but justify and have grace for my own shortcomings?
- Do I have impossible expectations for myself? Do I have no expectations? Why?
- Do I have a victim mentality? Do I feel everyone is against me? Am I filled with self-pity? What is my part in that?
- Am I constantly fixing people, situations, or problems? What are the consequences of fixing other people instead of myself?
- Am I always trying to be in charge? Do I get upset when I don't get my way?
- Do I struggle with sexuality? Do I understand God's plan for sex? Am I trying to get love and acceptance through sex? Do I use sex to manipulate?
- Do I see God as loving or mean? How can I change my attitude toward God?
- Do I take on responsibilities that are not mine? Why or why not?
- Do I feel responsible for someone else's growth? How?

Character Checklist

Please remember that while these traits are listed as "positive" and "negative", it can be negative to be overboard in a "positive" trait. For example, we can be overly responsible and take responsibility for attitudes, behaviors, and situations that are not ours to take; or "help" others in an effort to fix or control them. Please feel free to tailor these traits to your own situation. Since we usually fall somewhere in between, it is helpful to consider the percentage of the trait we possess. For example: you may be 80% trustworthy and 20% prone to gossip. If we do periodic reviews of our character traits, over a period of time we will be pleased to see how much progress we've made. You may want to date this for that purpose.

"Positive" traits	%	"Negative" traits	%
Aware of others		Self-centered	
Helpful to others		Self-indulgent	
Generous		Selfish	
Thoughtful		Self-pitying	
Open-minded, gracious		Smug, stubborn	
Constructively critical		Judgmental	
Respectful		Disrespectful	
Patient		Impatient	
Tolerant		Intolerant	
Realistic		Unrealistic	
Assertive		Submissive	
Cooperative		Domineering	
Outgoing		Withdrawn	
Forgiving		Resentful	
Trusting		Suspicious	
Trustworthy		Prone to gossip	
Content		Envious	
Agreeable		Disagreeable	
Cheerful		Depressed	
Courteous		Discourteous	
Kind		Unkind	
Loving, caring		Indifferent	
Discreet		Lacking discretion	
Stable		Panicky, violent	
Consistent		Inconsistent	
Sincere		Insincere	
Honest		Dishonest	
Willing to admit faults		Self-righteous	
Humble		Arrogant	
Calm		Worrisome	
Relaxed		Tense	
Confident, having faith		Fearful, apprehensive	
Hopeful		Despondent	
Optimistic		Pessimistic	
Living in today		Living in the past, worrying about the future	
Industrious		Lazy	
Prompt, on time		Procrastinating, late	
Purposeful		Aimless	
Responsible		Irresponsible	
Using talents and abilities		Disinterested in self	
Thankful		Ungrateful	
Willing to seek change and improve		Smug, complacent	

RELATED SCRIPTURE

Look over the following verses. Write any thoughts in the space provided or in a separate notebook.

Psalm 139:1-18, 23-24

Matthew 23:1-28

Mark 14:27-31, 66-72 and John 21:15-17

2 Corinthians 13:5

Ephesians 4:20-32

Colossians 2:13-23, 3:5-10

1 John 4:20-21

A few more verses on this subject:
Jeremiah 17:9-10, Lamentations 3:19-23, Lamentations 3:40, Romans 2:1-4, Galatians 6:4-5, Ephesians 5:1-20, James 1:19-26

Thoughts

Thoughts

Thoughts

Thoughts

Restoration

Walking the Path Part I

Restore my relationship with God by admitting my stuff, submitting each piece to Him, and allowing Him to lead me (because I found areas where my stuff was keeping me off the path).

Some of you have some red flags going up at the mention of us restoring our relationship with God. It seems almost sacrilegious. God is the only one who can restore our relationship with Him, and that's true to a point. There's nothing we can do to gain salvation, Jesus had to do all the work and provide the way. That's true. All we have to do is accept Jesus' sacrifice in our place and He forgives every sin, past, present, and future. Nothing we do can ever separate us from that salvation.

There is, however, a school of thought out there that says that since we can't do anything on our own, any work on our part is striving to earn our salvation. Yet James writes in James 2:14, "What's the use of saying you have faith if you don't prove it by your actions?" As I said in the first chapter, if it is God alone who makes us follow His will, then why aren't we perfect at the moment of salvation? If we aren't responsible for our actions, who is? God? Why is He having so much trouble fixing you? That may sound harsh, but *you* are responsible for your thoughts and actions. God will tell you His will and give you the strength to do it. You are responsible for seeking His will and following it.

We have choices. God constantly tells us to obey, do, follow, turn from, think, and believe. We choose whether or not we obey, do, follow, turn from, think, and believe. Every day we choose to follow God or follow our selfish desires. We must choose to pursue the will of God summed up in the first two commandments: love (trust) Him and love others. We must choose whether or not we trust God enough to look at our stuff and submit it to Him. What kind of relationship do we have with Him if we keep hiding our stuff from Him? Doing that breaks our relationship with Him. We must restore our side. We must turn from our destructive ways. We must quit rebelling and follow Him. We must submit our stuff.

Hopefully you have already begun to examine your stuff, but even if you haven't you still need to know what happens next because this is where the healing starts. This is where we begin to experience true freedom. Remember what 1 John 1:9 says, "But if we confess our sins to Him, He is faithful and just to forgive us and to cleanse us from every wrong." This is where we confess every wrong, repent, and allow God to forgive us and lead us on the path. Again, it is not our eternal salvation that is in question, this is about the depth of our relationship with Him.

When you finish your honest examination of your stuff you will have a pretty good idea of where you are. You will see areas where you don't trust God and where you have hurt other people and/or yourself. Now is the time to admit them and submit them to God. Remember when God called to Adam, "Where are you?" Adam replied, "I heard you, so I hid. I was afraid because I was naked." That's exactly what we need to do as well. Adam admitted he was hiding and what the root cause was. Granted, he blows it with his answer to the next question by blaming the fruit-eating on Eve, but at least he admits that he ate it! Progress, not perfection!

Psalm 32:3-9 gives us an amazing picture of restoration:

> When I refused to confess my sin, I was weak and miserable, and I
> groaned all day long. Day and night your hand of discipline was heavy
> on me. My strength evaporated like water in the summer heat.
>
> Finally, I confessed all my sins to you and stopped trying to hide them. I said to myself,
> "I will confess my rebellion to the Lord." And you forgave me! All my guilt is gone.
>
> Therefore, let all the godly confess their rebellion to you while there is time,
> that they may not drown in the floodwaters of judgement. For you are my hiding
> place; you protect me from trouble. You surround me with songs of victory.
>
> The Lord says, "I will guide you along the best pathway for your life.
> I will advise you and watch over you. Do not be like a senseless horse
> or mule that needs a bit and bridle to keep it under control.

Restoring our relationship with God means more than just saying we're sorry. How many times have you confessed a sin and told God you wouldn't do it again, only to find yourself confessing the same thing a week later? Confession is only the beginning of submitting our stuff to God. It is vital that we *agree with God* that what we did or believed was wrong or hurtful. Many times we're only sorry for the outcome of our actions. Deep down, we're still thinking we can do things our way and get better results. Until we can agree that whatever we were thinking/doing was damaging our life and relationships we will keep believing/doing it. When we agree with God that His way is better He will begin to change us.

This can be hard for many of us because we are so good at justifying our behavior. If we have defense mechanisms or walls of protection it will be hard to give them up and trust God. They served a purpose when we were lost in the woods. Now, hard as it may be, we must admit that they've kept us off the path. Like Adam, we must admit what we can and keep working on the rest. God's kingdom is upside down compared to this world. Vengeance, control, selfishness, criticism, arrogance, stubbornness, and disrespect (to name a few) may seem natural if we've fallen in with the culture around us. But God's way is to bless your enemies, submit, give, turn the other cheek, love, forgive, respect, be humble, and let Him defend you. That is not to say that you let abuse happen by any means. But it does mean we see the folly of responding and reacting the way the world does.

Group Discussion: What have you struggled with over and over again even though you've apologized to God? How do you think agreeing with God about your stuff will make a difference in your life?

When we're done confessing and agreeing that our stuff kept us off the path and ruined parts of our lives, we must submit our stuff to God. He is the one who takes it away and leads us in a new direction. In the examination example where the wife is writing about her husband it might look like this: "God, I realize that I've been selfish with my husband. I've been concerned about myself and my happiness and not thinking of his happiness. I see that this has caused problems in our relationship. I don't want to be selfish anymore because I agree with You that it hurts me and my relationships. I also agree that it hurts my relationship with You because I'm not trusting You with my happiness. Please take away my selfishness. I submit it to you. Help me to recognize it when it rears its ugly head and give me the wisdom and strength to resist it. I want to focus more on my husband's happiness. Please give me the desire to be giving towards him. The truth is I find my satisfaction in You."

After we have confessed our stuff to God, agreed that it was damaging, submitted it to Him, and asked Him to remove it and change our hearts we must do one more thing. In the beginning I said that our stuff has power over us when we hide it. Confessing it to God is vital because He is our most important relationship and He is the only one who can eternally *forgive* our stuff. But it still keeps our stuff a secret in our day to day life, and Satan will use those secrets to lure us off the path through fear of exposure. We are eternally secure in Jesus' forgiveness, but we can continue to live in the brokenness of hiding, avoiding, and denying with other people. That's hypocrisy. In order to be entirely free and healed we must confess to *another person*! I know, the idea is cringe-worthy! But in James 5:16 we are commanded to, "Confess your sins to *each other* and pray for each other so that you may be *healed*."

There is something extremely powerful about admitting all your stuff to someone else who accepts you regardless of what you've done. It's like staring down Satan, face to face, and snapping the chains of your past right before his eyes! Or pulling that huge magnet out of your pocket and throwing it in his face! Boom! Suddenly you can move, your compass works, and you're free! Those beliefs and actions that you discovered were harming yourself and others don't carry the same weight they once did. Satan will try to throw them back at you again and again, but each time you confess them to another human being their power diminishes and you get stronger and stronger. As Paul says, "I am glad to boast about my weaknesses, so that the power of Christ may work through me." (2 Corinthians 12:9)

> Group Discussion: Do you cringe at the thought of confessing your stuff to someone else? Why? Is it God's will? Could it be powerful in your life? How? How do you think you will feel when you're done?

We think we're so alone! We think others will despise us if they knew our true selves. Well, they're thinking the same thing! When you tell others your story, the truth is that they'll probably be able to relate and tell you that they've been there too (if they're honest). "But remember that the temptations that come into your life are no different from what others experience" (1 Corinthians 10:13). How liberating to be able to share our true selves with another person and have them love and accept us anyway! What a gift to be able to do that for someone else!

When you share your stuff make sure it's with someone who is going through this process, too, in some way, shape, or form. Someone who is humble and truly knows the importance of confession. Many of us have been burned by someone we thought we could trust. We told something that we just couldn't keep inside anymore, and instead of giving grace, that person told others, judged and lectured us, or stopped hanging out with us. They made us want to hide even more. They made God's will even more difficult for us to follow! Yikes! Don't confess to that person, and don't be that person.

Restore your relationship with God by confessing to Him, agreeing with Him, submitting to Him, and doing things His way – which includes confessing to another person. Just like baptism is an outward sign that you trust God to forgive your stuff, confessing to another person is an outward sign that you trust God to heal your stuff. I won't lie, it's scary the first time because you don't know for sure what will happen. But if you trust God you will do it.

LOCATION CHECK

You may read through and discuss these suggestions, questions, and verses as a group, but they are meant for you to work through in detail on your own. You don't have to do every suggestion, answer every question, or read every verse. Just focus on the ones that speak to you. There is room at the end of this chapter to write your thoughts if you wish.

SUGGESTIONS

Find a time when you can be alone for an extended period of time. First, thank God for your identity in Christ and your strengths. God says in Psalm 50:23 that "giving thanks is a sacrifice that truly honors Me." Then confess, agree, and submit your stuff to God. If you find an area you are still justifying, talk to a trusted friend and pray for God's insight.

Find a person you can confess your stuff to. You want a person who is humble, honest with their stuff, and willing to listen and encourage without giving advice or judgement. It could be someone in your group, a friend, or a pastor. Explain what you are doing and what you expect from them if they are not familiar with this concept. (If you get any push back at this point, find someone else!) Set aside a few hours in a confidential place to confess your location, your stuff, your part in your problems. If you can't find anyone you trust in your immediate circle, go to a priest. They are used to hearing confession and won't be surprised at anything. The point is to confess, get it out, stop hiding, and admit your stuff out loud to another human being.

QUESTIONS

The following questions are designed to help jumpstart your thinking.

- Am I afraid to admit my faults to God? Why?
- How do I feel about confessing my stuff to another person?
- Are there areas of my life where am I can be completely honest?
- Do I believe that honestly admitting my stuff brings healing? Why or why not?
- If I do not feel ready to confess, do I need to do more work on humility, trust, and honesty?
- Could I start this process by confessing the stuff I can admit now and work on the rest over time?
- Can I admit that I am not perfect? How can I quit trying to be?
- How do I try to justify or dismiss hurt I may have caused others?
- Do I know anyone I can confess my stuff to? Why do I trust him or her?
- Do I have trouble with the concept of trusting someone with my stuff? Who could I talk to about these fears?
- Does my desire to be a perfect Christian keep me from believing someone could accept me unconditionally after hearing my stuff? How?

- What have I learned about myself by determining the root causes of my problems and actions?
- Have I isolated myself from others? How could confessing to another person help me?
- Is there one thing I don't want anyone else to know? Could I start with that?
- Has there been a time when someone confessed something to me and I accepted them?
- How did I feel after confessing to God and another person? Is anything different? Better?
- What, if anything, have I left out?

RELATED SCRIPTURE

Look over the following verses. How do they affect your thoughts on confession?

Job 42:1-6

Psalm 32:3-5

Psalm 51

Proverbs 28:13

Isaiah 29:15-16

Luke 15:17-24

James 4:7-10

A few more verses on this subject:
Jeremiah 14:20, Lamentations 3:19-22, Romans 3:23, James 5:16, I John 1:8-10

Thoughts

Thoughts

Restoration

Walking the Path Part II

*And restore my relationships with others by making amends with people I've
hurt and forgiving those who've hurt me (because this is God's path).*

The two greatest commandments: Love (trust) God and love your neighbor. In the last chapter we learned that loving God means trusting Him with all our stuff, submitting it all to Him. This chapter deals with the second most important commandment. In fact it's so important it's almost permanently attached to the first. It's loving other people. May I suggest that the state of your personal relationships is *no small thing to God?* Jesus says, "So if you are standing before the altar in the Temple, offering a sacrifice to God, and you suddenly remember that someone has something against you, leave your sacrifice there before the altar. Go and be reconciled to that person. Then come and offer your sacrifice to God." (Matt. 5:23-24)

What is Jesus really saying there? Take a minute to think about that. You cannot be the cause of pain in someone else's life and then worship God like nothing is wrong. Our love for God is tied to how we treat others. When we hurt them, intentionally or not, and refuse to make it right, what we're really saying is that the other person doesn't matter as much as we do. We have the audacity to think that our relationships don't matter when we come before the throne of God! Jesus says that they *do* matter – in fact, they matter *more* than our faithfulness in worshipping Him! He actually wants you to put Him, the God of the Universe, on hold and go restore the relationship you have strained. He values our relationships with each other that much!

Most of us hurt people unintentionally. In a world filled with unique individuals we're bound to have misunderstandings and conflicts of interest. Here's the bottom line: If you know there's a breach or even suspect there's some hurt in any relationship, you are personally responsible for making it right as much as it depends on you. To do less and still come boldly to the throne is hypocrisy. I'm going to mix the NIV and NLT translations of Proverbs 14:9 for a minute: "Fools mock at making amends for sin (NIV), but the godly acknowledge it and seek reconciliation (NLT)."

Having said all that, most of the time you should not rush to reconcile with someone without thinking it through first. Relationships and circumstances can be complicated and you don't want to act prematurely and become the cause of more harm. You may be in the middle of a hurtful relationship right now and the last thing you want to do is reconcile. It may be 90% the other person's fault. You may need time to get your head clear before you can approach someone. Some relationships are abusive and actually need severing. Before you rush out to check the "made amends" box off your list, take time to make sure you know what you're making amends for and your motivation behind the amends. I believe God will honor your intention to reconcile as soon as you are ready. Jesus didn't add, "unless they hurt you first," to the end of the verse above! The goal is always to get to a place where we can take responsibility for our side of things and love the other person, whether it includes continued contact with them or not.

Again, the way we treat people is directly tied to our love for God. Benson puts it this way,

> Shall we say, then, that if a man first loves God he will then spontaneously love his neighbor? The New Testament reverses the order. "He that loveth not his brother whom he hath seen, cannot love God whom he hath not seen…" A cherished resentment, a harboured [sic] grudge, an unforgiving spirit, an unconfessed wrong so put the soul out of focus that we cannot see God, but God became immediately real to many of us when we made restitution for wrongs done to others.[5]

It's only by loving others that we fully understand, express, and demonstrate our love for God. Yet haven't we been okay with a certain level of friction and grudge-holding in our relationships? Don't we have an unwillingness to admit when we've offended someone or a knee-jerk blaming of others for our reactions? "If you hadn't said that then I wouldn't have done this!" Hopefully you've exposed any of that attitude lurking in your stuff.

This is the point where you look back through the stuff in your life (which is why it's important to write it down) and look at *your part* of the hurt in your relationships. The goal here is to clean up your side of the street, so to speak. Maybe you did something really rude and hurtful to your brother ten years ago. Maybe you've moved past it, but you've never acknowledged you were wrong and made it right. Now is the time to get rid of that baggage in your relationship. He may or may not respond well depending on the state of your relationship today, but *sincerely* acknowledging that your actions caused pain removes the incident from *your* bag of stuff (hopefully from his, too, but that's *his* responsibility, not yours!). You basically sweep that piece of garbage off of your side of the street. You keep doing that with all your relationships, past and present (yes, really), and eventually when you look around there won't be a bunch of unresolved past relationship stuff lingering around and tainting your present relationships.

> Group Discussion: Does someone have something against you? Can you think of a past hurt that you've never taken responsibility for? Do you sense that it is affecting your relationship with that person? With God? How?

Let's talk about this term "amends." It encapsulates so much more than just an apology. It's easy to say, "Sorry," and then continue the same behavior. We need to have some skin in the game, so to speak. We must restore the trust that was broken. We must actively pursue the change God is producing in us. That means we verbally acknowledge to the other person our part in the conflict, that we were wrong, and what we will do to make it right. In the example above, you might say, "Hey, Bro, you know years ago when I did X to you? I know that really hurt you and I just want to say that I was wrong and that I'm really sorry. Will you forgive me?" You also fix, replace, or pay for any damages you've caused, just like Zacchaeus did (Luke 19:1-10). We do this face to face if at all possible, not saving our pride, but in humility and confidence in God's forgiveness.

If we can't do it face to face then we do the next best thing, either on the phone, a video calling app (or whatever new technology is out there – hologram?), or in a letter or email. Texting seems like a cop-out—too brief and impersonal, but you'll have to decide if that's appropriate. We may not be able to make some amends directly. Maybe that person is dead, or the business closed, or we may have been asked not to contact someone ever again. In this case, you can write a letter and read it to a trusted friend. Or, you can volunteer at an organization which has some meaning to the situation. For instance, if you have treated a grandparent poorly and they are no longer living, you can volunteer at a nursing home as a form of reconciliation. If you can no longer pay someone back because you do not know their whereabouts, you may choose to make a donation to a charity as a form of restitution. Shelters, hospitals, or serving at church could serve a similar purpose. Changed behavior towards others can be a form of amends as well. You may vow to never hurt another person with the same bad behavior.

Let me be clear, these are not actions we take in order to be forgiven by God or work for our salvation. They are simply a sign to ourselves of the changes God has made within us and our inward commitment to walk the path and do things differently. They are our skin in the game, our doing of the Word, our faith in action.

So here's how this works. Once you have identified a person or institution you need to make amends to you pray about it (or maybe you need to ask God to show you who those people are). Ask God to give you insight to be sure you are taking full responsibility for your part and nothing more. Then run it by a friend who knows what you're trying to do and agrees with it. It's easy to lose perspective when we're in the middle of a conflict. We may have trouble seeing what is and is not our responsibility. We might unwittingly be making the amends to feel good about ourselves at someone else's expense. This isn't about humiliating ourselves, making others feel good at our expense, or setting ourselves up for abuse. A friend can help us wade through all that and make sure our motivation is pure.

When you're ready, or when God brings someone into your life (surprise!), you seek to restore the relationship from your end only. You focus on your actions and restitution only. You don't build up or rehearse or put expectations on how the other person will respond. Sometimes people respond well and a friendship is healed, sometimes you are rejected and the relationship is ended. Sometimes it takes time and consistency for trust to be rebuilt. If you have caused deep, deep pain for someone, you may have to assure them of your amends several times and for several years before you have earned their trust again. You don't get to dictate the consequences of your actions. The other person's response is not your responsibility. You are to just "do your part to live in peace with everyone, as much as possible." (Romans 12:18)

> Group Discussion: Can you think of at least one person you need to make amends to? Can you share the circumstance with the group? What do you think would happen if you attempted to restore this relationship? How can you let those expectations go?

Another important aspect of restoring a relationship is forgiveness. When Jesus taught us to pray He told us to ask God to "forgive us our sins just as we have forgiven those who have sinned against us." (Matt. 6:12) Forgiveness flows out of our gratefulness for God's forgiveness in our own lives.

In Luke Chapter 7 a woman with a bad reputation comes to Jesus at Simon's house and washes his feet with her tears, dries them with her hair, and puts expensive perfume on them. Simon questions why Jesus would let her do that since she was an immoral woman. Jesus proceeds to tell a story about two men who were lent money, one 500 pieces of silver and one 50. But neither could repay the lender so he canceled both their debts. Jesus asks Simon which man loved the lender more after that. Simon replies that the man with the larger debt probably did. Jesus then says that Simon is right and He refers to the woman at his feet: "I tell you, her sins—and they are many—have been forgiven, so she has shown me much love. But a person who is forgiven little shows only a little love (v. 47)."

If we don't think we have sinned much, we won't be able to love much. Let that sink in. If we don't think we have sinned much, we won't be able to love much! When we truly grasp the enormity of our *own* personal sins and the incredible love Jesus has for us that He would die to forgive us *while we were still sinners*, then we can begin to look at others differently – with grace for *their* faults. All of us are only human. We all have stuff. The bottom line is that God commands us to forgive.

Forgiveness is a decision we make, not an emotion we feel. We decide to release another person's hold on our life. We decide to stop letting that situation eat away at us. Forgiveness does not mean we must accept unacceptable behavior or open ourselves up to abuse. We do not put ourselves in dangerous situations or reestablish harmful relationships. You don't need to go around telling everyone who's hurt you, "You know that thing you did that really hurt me? I forgive you." That smacks of pride and will probably cause more conflict (that's not an absolute; God may very well lead you to do that, but it will be in love and humility). Forgiveness is more about keeping ourselves free of bitterness than it is about making others feel good or bad. We do it for our own benefit. If someone else is blessed by our change in attitude, that is a bonus.

We make the decision to forgive, we tell ourselves we forgive, we act like we forgive, and eventually the feelings of forgiveness will come. We must start with the decision, not the feeling. If we wait for the feelings to come, they never will. We must act our way into a new way of thinking, and the feelings will follow. As always, we pray that God would work in our hearts.

One person you probably need to restore your relationship with but is often overlooked is yourself. When you examined your stuff you were probably surprised and disappointed at your part of the problems, conflicts, resentments, and frustrations, and the at root causes of those thoughts and actions. We hurt ourselves when we act at odds with our values and ideals. When we damage relationships with people we love we also get hurt in the process. That's part of the reason we don't want to look at our stuff. It's painful. Some of us have treated ourselves terribly in our attempt to make up for our mistakes. Others of us hurt ourselves by trying to deflect or ignore them. Wherever you fall on that scale it's important to tell yourself you're sorry for taking off on a path that hurt you and forgive yourself so you can live at peace with yourself.

Group Discussion: What do you think about the idea of forgiving yourself? What are some things you need to forgive yourself for?

LOCATION CHECK

You may read through and discuss these suggestions, questions, and verses as a group, but they are meant for you to work through in detail on your own. You don't have to do every suggestion, answer every question, or read every verse. Just focus on the ones that speak to you. There is room at the end of this chapter to write your thoughts if you wish.

SUGGESTIONS

Make two lists, one for people to whom you owe amends and one for those you need to forgive. You may choose to divide each list into three columns: yes, maybe, and never; or now, later, and never. List the person and the reason next to them. You may have several reasons for one person and one person may be listed in each column for different offenses if necessary. Ask God to guide you in carrying out the restoration of these relationships.

When preparing to make amends, run the offense, what you will say, and your expectations by a trusted friend who agrees with what you are doing to check your motivation and expectations. If they express concern, ask God for more guidance and humility. After the amends are made, tell your friend how it went and ask for feedback.

When forgiving and making amends to yourself, you may find it freeing to face yourself in the mirror and forgive yourself point by point. You may write all your hurtful behavior down on separate pieces of paper and burn them one by one. Or you may make a list and keep it so when Satan tries to condemn you again you can point to it and say, "I'm forgiven!" However you choose to handle forgiving yourself, it is vital for you to realize that you are only human and give yourself the same grace you now offer to others.

QUESTIONS

The following questions are designed to help jumpstart your thinking.

- Am I willing to make amends and forgive? If not, why not?
- Have I rationalized or justified my behavior to avoid making amends?
- What part does God play in my amends? In forgiving others?
- Who do I need to make amends to or forgive first? Why haven't I done it yet?
- What am I going to say in my direct amends to take responsibility only for my part and avoid blaming anyone or anything else?
- If I decide not to make amends in person, how can I make sure I'm not just saving my pride?
- If there is someone on my list who I will never be able to contact, how can I demonstrate my amends and forgiveness?
- How can I forgive without accepting unacceptable behavior?
- Why does God command me to forgive others?

- How can I forgive someone who has not stopped causing harm?
- How can I forgive someone who does not acknowledge that they wronged me?
- How can I forgive myself for all the difficulties I've caused myself? What can I do this week to begin my amends to myself?
- If I have people on my 'maybe' and 'never' list, how can I move them to the 'yes' or 'now' list?

RELATED SCRIPTURE

Look over the following verses. How do they help you have the courage to make amends and forgive?

Ezekiel 33:14-16

Matthew 5:23-24

Matthew 5:43-48

Matthew 6:14-15

Luke 19:8

Romans 13:8

1John 4:18-21

More verses on this subject:
Matthew 5:25-26, Mark 11:25, Luke 6:27-36, Romans 12: 17-21, Romans 15:5-7, Ephesians 4:2, Ephesians 4:31-32, 1 Thessalonians 5:11, 1 Peter 4:8, 1 John 4:11-12

Thoughts

Thoughts

Fellowship

Helping Others Wake Up

*I share my experience with others, both for their encouragement and my humility
(because someone else's sharing helped me wake up in the woods).*

Once we know where we are we sure don't want to get lost again, do we? We don't want to go back to hiding our stuff, because as soon as we do that Satan can start using it against us. We'll start separating ourselves from others, becoming less open and honest. We'll take our eyes off the path and focus on the trees and rocks until we're lost in our pride, fear, anger, and selfishness again. Sharing your stuff with others is essential to walking the path – it is the opposite of hiding. If confession frees us and heals us, then we need a place where we can continue to share our experiences on a regular basis.

Fellowship is what makes sharing possible.

First, let me say that "fellowship" is not my favorite word. It brings up visions of a bunch of uptight people with cheesy smiles milling around the church gym at a pot-luck pretending to be interested in each other but in reality only making stupid small talk and trying to look like they have it all together. That's not appealing. That's appalling! Church can be a very lonely place.

Again, Benson nails it: "'It is pitiable,' as Dr. James Denny once said, 'to see the substitutes that are found for fellowship in the Church and the importance which is given them, only because the real thing is not there'... Little by little we have laid too much stress on the formal means of worship, to the neglect of that fellowship wherein the door of loneliness swings open and faith is fed in kindly company with those who had fears and hopes and sins like our own, but have found happy victory".[6]

Have we substituted programs for personal relationships? Have we made people projects instead of friends? Have we turned church into a checklist?

I sang – check
I prayed – check
I gave – check

Have we decided that hanging out is not spiritual fellowship if there's no Bible reading or prayer; as if Jesus wouldn't hang out where people are just having fun getting to know one another? If you have Jesus in you, how could He not be there? Jesus said that people will know you are His disciples if you love each other (John 13:35). Making people feel loved and important and accepted *is* spiritual! It's #2 on the commandment list. How can we encourage "those who had fears and hopes and sins like our own" if we don't know people and aren't honest with them?

We need each other! We need to be real! Most of all, we need to demonstrate the grace of God *in the flesh!* We must be Christ to each other. As Christians, the atmosphere we want to create is one of grace and forgiveness, not perfection and pride. We must rip off the fake Jesus mask we created to hide our hurt and struggles. That mask only repels others who are hurting and keeps us isolated from each other. There is no hiding from Jesus and we shouldn't create an atmosphere where others feel the need to hide from us. Instead, we must create an atmosphere where sin is powerless because Jesus forgives it. In a sense we need to destigmatize sin, not so we can glory in it, ignore it, or minimize the hurt it causes, but so that it loses its power to paralyze. We can turn our perception of it from this pile of radioactive waste that can only be handled with a hazmat suit to a piece of dirt that Jesus can flick from our shoulder. "Neither do I condemn you," Jesus declared. "Go now and leave your life of sin." (John 8:11 NIV)

The Apostle Paul was great at sharing. When you read the letters he wrote he is constantly talking about how lost he was and how Jesus found him and rescued him. He shares about wrestling with current struggles. Paul even goes so far as to say he boasts in his weakness because that is when Jesus' strength is on full display in his life. He reveals that God refused to take a thorn (hurt, problem, struggle?) away from him. Instead, God told him that His grace would be enough for Paul to deal with it. I don't know about you, but that makes me feel better!

When you share both your current hurts and struggles and your victories over past problems you give hope to others. Hope that they are not alone, and hope that they can overcome their hurts. How many of you have heard a sermon and afterward felt like the pastor was speaking directly to you? You know, a pastor is not the only one who can do that. We can do that with each other. Every time we share a struggle there's the potential to connect with someone experiencing a similar struggle. Every time we share how God healed a hurt there's a chance that we give hope to another with a similar hurt. We are living in the light of God's presence, and I John 1:7 says that when we do that we have fellowship with each other.

An important interjection here: You don't have to (and probably shouldn't) share all the personal details of your struggles with a group like you did when you confessed them to a trusted friend (you did go into detail there, right?). Some aspects of our sin are not appropriate to share in a group setting. We should not glory in the gory details. We only need to share enough to be real about what Jesus healed us from, or what we are struggling to submit to Him. Pray about it. Let Jesus guide you as you walk this path. He'll tell you what is and is not appropriate to share. Save the details for your trusted friend.

If you've done the work of examining your stuff and confessing it to someone, and if you've made some amends and forgiven some people, chances are you have some pretty big stories to tell about God's hand in your life. That's exciting! Someone needs to hear that so they can have hope for their stuff! And—*News Flash*—you're going to continue to experience problems in the future. As those problems come up you're going to need to hear someone else's experience so you can be encouraged.

In the book "The Purpose Driven Life", Rick Warren says, "…your most effective ministry will come out of your deepest hurts. The things you're most embarrassed about, most ashamed of, and most reluctant to share are the very tools God can use most powerfully to heal others."[7] *That* is how we help others – by sharing our experience of discovering and submitting our stuff to God. For some of us the thought of sharing may bring up old feelings of worthlessness. Your insecurity may discourage you from being a trusted friend to someone who needs you. Please don't think you have nothing to offer to others. That diminishes the value of Jesus' grace in your life. Instead, trust God with sharing your stuff.

> Group Discussion: What is your area of deepest hurt? Can you share that with others? How could that help you continue to heal?

At this point, you may be tempted to start doling out advice, to take responsibility for someone else's growth, to try to fix and control others, or to start throwing stones (John 8:1-9). Before we go on, let's define what it means to throw stones. Obviously it doesn't mean the same as it did in Jesus' day. We don't kill someone with rocks. The book of Job is a great illustration of what it means to throw stones of judgment. I suggest reading it sometime with that in mind. Basically, Job's friends tried to help him by figuring out just what Job had done to cause his problems, or what God wanted him to learn from them. Their advice sounds a lot like many Christians today. But God said in Job 42:7, "I am angry with you (Eliphaz) and your two friends, for you have not been right about Me, as my servant Job was." God was angry!

It's so easy for us to look at someone else's life and judge the cause and the cure. Definitive phrases like, "You just need to…", "You know what you should do is…", "If you'd only…", "If you hadn't…", "Why can't you…", or (watch out for the lightning bolt) "God told me to tell you…" are big, fat rocks we pick up and hurl at people when we think we have more spiritual insight than they do about their own lives. Job's friends couldn't comprehend that the reason Job was suffering was simply that God is sovereign—He is the ultimate authority and everything He does is right. May I suggest that we don't have all the answers for other people? We hardly have all the answers for our own lives.

So, resist those temptations to fix, control, and "should" on others. That's your stuff trying to weasel its way back in. Galatians 6:1 says, "Dear brothers and sisters, if another Christian is overcome by some sin, you who are godly should gently and humbly help that person back onto the right path. And be careful not to fall into the same temptation yourself."

Gentleness. Humility. Care. All acquired by examining and submitting your stuff. Remember, if you "help" someone who is off the path without knowing your own location, you're bound to end up miles off the path yourself. Respect them in their struggle. Ask questions instead of giving answers. Share what you've learned and been through and let God do the work. After all, we didn't heal ourselves and we can't heal anyone else. We had to let God do for us what we could not do for ourselves! We had to submit our stuff to Him because we couldn't carry it anymore, and we can't carry anyone else's stuff.

Another note of caution: some of you will be tempted to get legalistic and formulaic with sharing. Don't worry if someone shares off topic, or not at all. Forcing people to share when they're not ready is controlling. Relax! You can't force true fellowship.

What you *can* do is invite others to your group to come and see if this really is a better way to live and to walk the path alongside you. Did I say invite? What I meant was invite, invite, invite, INVITE! Be an example. Go first. Create an atmosphere where sharing is safe and normal and healing and others will be attracted to it like a moth to a flame. Don't worry about the theology of what others share. They're walking their own path with God. You have no idea what journey God is having them walk through on the inside. You don't know their heart. God does. If you critique what they share you can bet they won't be back. They'll be crushed and embarrassed and they won't share again. They'll feel judged and rejected. They'll close themselves off to growth. I sure don't want to be the cause of that in someone else's life.

Yes, the Bible "is useful for teaching, rebuking, correcting and training" (I Timothy 3:16). After the meeting, in a private conversation, you might say, "Hey! I appreciated what you shared. I know some places in the Bible that talk more about that if you'd like to get together sometime. If not, that's okay. I'm just glad you're here." It's the freedom of sharing, whether it's theologically correct or not, that opens us up to learning and growth. Allowing people to be open and honest and, yes, wrong about some theology allows them to be open to hearing and accepting the truth. I know that rubs some of you the wrong way, but it is not your job to fix people! It's God's. Hasn't your own understanding of life and God changed over the last several years? Allow others the same grace in growth that God has given you.

You can't force people to become disciples. A disciple is someone who follows Jesus voluntarily. How did Jesus cause people to follow Him? By loving and accepting people where they were. He loved Zacchaeus by dining at his house *before* Zacchaeus made any changes. He rescued the woman caught in adultery from being shamed and stoned *before* she changed her ways. He loved the man born blind by healing him *before* the man even knew who Jesus was. He laid down his life for you *before* you quit sinning. Follow Jesus' example. Make disciples by loving people where they are. Change will come as they follow Him.

Let others hear how Jesus is working in your life and let God connect the dots. They'll hear what you (or someone else, your story won't connect with everyone) have to say and they'll relate to it. They'll hear how Jesus worked or is working, that you're making progress, and they'll think it'd be nice to talk to you about their struggle because you'll understand and not condemn them. Then they'll strike up a conversation with you and you won't just dole out advice, but you'll be interested in their struggle. Then you'll have more conversations and you'll share what worked for you. They may or may not agree, but you love them and keep getting together with them because they matter and they remain open because you're not judging and fixing, you're loving!

You continue to understand because you were once where they are in this area, and you're exactly where they are in some other area. Because of that you keep sharing what worked for you without saying, "what you should do is…" and they remain open and *God* is working in their heart. You will learn things about your life from them as they share how God is uniquely working in their life. Maybe God leads you to share a hard truth with them, but it will be in the context of this loving friendship you've established where you've earned the right to speak into their life because you've demonstrated acceptance and love for them *as they are*. Even if they reject the hard truth you keep loving, accepting, and understanding them with humility. This is how true fellowship plays out. This is how we help and encourage one another. This is how iron sharpens iron - not by banging away at each other, but by rubbing shoulders as we experience life together. It's called *friendship!*

People are dying to be loved and accepted for real! We want to be wanted. You, at your core, crave authentic relationships. That's how God made us: "It is not good for man to be alone." But very few of us will invite ourselves into a group unless we are desperate. Please, don't let anyone be desperate. Don't ignore a fellow human being lost in the woods of their stuff when you have found that examining your stuff, submitting it to God, and confessing it leads to the Path. Invite others to be a part of your group, then invite more and split, then invite more and split! Of course, you will have only a small group of intimate friends—you can't be everyone's best friend, but be open to new people. No, you can't force anyone else to wake up, but you can give anyone and everyone the opportunity for true fellowship. Don't huddle in your familiar friendships. Reach out. Branch out. Love God and love others. That *is* the path.

> Group Discussion: Would a group like this be welcome at your church? How could it work? Do you know anyone who would like to be involved? How can you encourage others to share their stories?

LOCATION CHECK

You may read through and discuss these suggestions, questions, and verses as a group, but they are meant for you to work through in detail on your own. You don't have to do every suggestion, answer every question, or read every verse. Just focus on the ones that speak to you. There is room at the end of this chapter to write your thoughts if you wish.

SUGGESTIONS

Think about what you have experienced as you have woken up, found your location, and been lead back to the path. Write them down or talk about them with a trusted friend.

Think about someone who would benefit from this journey. Write down some ways you can share it with them without preaching, controlling, pushing, or throwing stones.

Are there any areas of your life where you are still hiding? Write them down and pray about them. Write down some ways you could share these areas and receive help and encouragement from others.

QUESTIONS

The following questions are designed to help jumpstart your thinking.

- What is the most important concept this process has taught me? Can I share that with someone?
- Are there ways I can share what I've learned without talking? What are they?
- Was I encouraged by someone else in the group? What can I do to be an encouragement to others?
- What is the difference between sharing my story and giving advice?
- What was the response when I shared my experiences with others? What can I learn from that?
- How can I respond to a hurting person without trying to fix, manipulate, or control?
- How can I share at work? Is my job only about earning money, or is it an opportunity to share?
- What does the value of true fellowship say about my involvement in a small group? If I don't have a small group, how can I model true fellowship in my church family?
- What part has the group played in my growth?
- What principles have I learned from finding my location, submitting my stuff, and restoring my relationships? How can I explain them articulately?
- Am I a good example of a mature person? How?

RELATED SCRIPTURE

Look over the following verses. What do they say about the importance of fellowship and sharing?

Ecclesiastes 4:9-12

Mark 5:18-20

Luke 8:16-18

John 4:28-30, 39-41

John 9:1-38

Romans 10:14-15

1 John 1:5-10

More verses on this subject:
Psalm 50:15, Psalm 51:10-13, John 15:12-13, Romans 12:15, Romans 15:5, 1 Corinthians 12:25-26, Galatians 6:1-3, Ephesians 5:1-2, Philippians 4:10-14, Colossians 4:5-6, 1 Peter 3:15-16

Thoughts

Thoughts

Maturity

Checking My Location Daily

Evaluate my thoughts and actions on a daily basis to make sure I'm still following God to camp and not doing things my own way (because ignoring my location was what got me lost in the first place).

Let's remember where we were when we started this journey. We hurt ourselves and others without realizing it, we had bad habits we couldn't stop because we were unwilling to face them and let God remove them, we tried to control and manipulate, we put ourselves down because we couldn't see our good qualities, or we were prideful and self-righteous because we ignored our sin. Do we want to go back to that way of life? No!

> Group Discussion: Think back to your life before you started this process. Share how your view of yourself, others, and God has changed.

Just like following a map and compass to find camp in the real woods, we need to check our location frequently to make sure the cliff (problem) we just navigated around didn't knock us off course. 1 Peter 5:8 says, "Be careful! Watch out for the attacks from the Devil, your great enemy. He prowls around like a roaring lion, looking for some victim to devour." Like a predator stalking prey, Satan will try to sneak your stuff back into your life when you aren't paying attention. So pay attention! You can chose to live in Jesus' healing, or you can absentmindedly meander away. That's why we're encouraged to be on our guard, stay alert, and watch out (1 Thess 5:6, Mark 13:22-23, 1 Cor 10:12, Gal 6:1). If you have put forth the effort to honestly examine your stuff, submit and confess it, and make amends and forgive, and then declare that you're done, you are leaving your life open to the deception and denial you just eliminated.

So what does maturity look like? Well, first things first as they say. How can you follow Jesus if you don't know Him? Are you reading the Bible? Are you praying? How will you be able to distinguish Jesus' voice from Satan's if you aren't familiar with it? If you haven't read the Bible much, start with Matthew, Mark, Luke, and John to hear Jesus' actual words. Don't throw out the Old Testament just because it was before Jesus-in-the-flesh. Jesus is in there, too. Look that up if you didn't know it. It's fascinating! The entire Bible is about God and what He is like. His ways are not like ours so it would be really helpful to get His perspective!

There are a few places in the Bible where God says He will not hear our prayers. James 4:3 says, "And even when you do ask, you don't get it because your whole motive is wrong—you want only what will give you pleasure." I Peter 3:7b says, regarding husbands and wives, "If you don't treat her as you should, your prayers will not be heard." We need to pray to know God's will and let go of our own selfish desires, and we need to treat others the way God wants us to—leaving our gift at the altar and making amends. When we look for *God's* will when we pray we are infinitely more effective than if we pray for what *we* think is right. God will not only lead us to act as He wills, He will lead us to pray for others as He wills. *Then* our prayers will be powerful and effective! Prayer for knowledge of God's will keeps us from pushing ours.

Along with studying God's Word and praying, submit your day to God and ask Him to guide you every morning. In order to be lead we have to follow, right? We don't want to follow our own plans and desires. Think about this: your *best* thinking got you in some pretty messed up and painful situations. Your *highest* wisdom failed your relationships. Take a look back at your stuff if you forgot. That's not to say that life is perfect when we follow Jesus. This is not Heaven. People can be mean. Disasters happen. It's tough enough to trust God through these inevitable situations without adding your own selfishly-motivated solutions to the pile. So ask God for His wisdom and guidance and then look for it throughout the day.

Every night, evaluate your humility, trust, honesty, and restoration that day. Though it may seem overwhelming, it can be done in as little as 15 minutes. First, humble yourself before God and thank Him for providing for you. (There are several places in Psalms where God says that being truly grateful in your heart is more valuable than any sacrifice. That was *before* Jesus' death paid for our sins and the Israelites were still required to make all those sacrifices to cleanse themselves from sin. I find that an amazing concept.) Next, go over the events of the day and ask God to reveal what was good and what was bad. Ask Him, as David did, to examine your heart and see if you caused any offense or reacted in ungodly ways. Figure out the root cause of your wrongs and mistakes. Then immediately confess it and agree with God that it is wrong; submit it to Him and ask Him to remove it from your life. Restore any relationships by making amends as soon as possible. Choose to forgive people who hurt you to keep bitterness from creeping into your life. Also, be encouraged at any positive changes you see and thank God for them. There is a Daily Check Journal included at the end of this chapter. It includes some questions to help you get started with this discipline.

> Group Discussion: What do you think of the daily check concept? Is it overwhelming? Would you do it differently? Is it important to do it daily? Why?

You can also perform "spot checks" during the day whenever a difficult situation comes up or you're out of sorts and don't know why. Prayerfully ask yourselves some quick questions such as:

- Why am I feeling _____?
- Is this one of the root causes I struggle with?
- Is this true or right?
- What is my motivation at this moment?
- Is this my responsibility?
- What is my part?
- How can I respond differently?

After thinking for a moment about your thoughts and/or behavior you can choose to respond in a better way and make amends where you need to. You can also perform a spot check when you feel vulnerable. A helpful acronym to remember is H.A.L.T. Are you Hungry, Angry, Lonely, or Tired? Those are times when we all need to watch our behavior more closely.

It's also good to reevaluate your life once or twice a year. Get away for a while, whether it be to the bedroom or a remote cabin, and look at your life in detail. There are a few different ways to focus this evaluation. You can choose to examine your life over the last 6-12 months and see if any new patterns of behavior have shown up. You can also look at the stuff you already know about and evaluate the degree of change you see. You may take one problem in particular and focus on your behavior in that area over the past months. Or, you may choose to focus on one person or institution and evaluate that relationship. However you do it, taking the time to evaluate our lives from the distance of time gives us a perspective we cannot see on a daily basis.

Lastly, share in fellowship as often as possible. It keeps us humble and honest, it glorifies God, it helps and encourages others, and we are helped and encouraged by it as well.

Even though this journey has led us to wake up, find our location, and get on the path of God's will, we have not "arrived." We will never arrive at camp (complete maturity) until we are done with this earthly life. As you mature and grow you will notice areas you missed before and begin to work on them as well. Pain and imperfections will continue to be a part of your life. Have compassion on yourself. You'll be navigating this path for a lifetime. This is about progress, not perfection. Don't give up because you aren't able to overcome negative behavior immediately; God is working in you and leading you. Continue to be humble, trust God, and be honest with your problems and relationships, confessing, making amends, and forgiving and you will stay on the path.

LOCATION CHECK

You may read through and discuss these suggestions, questions, and verses as a group, but they are meant for you to work through in detail on your own. You don't have to do every suggestion, answer every question, or read every verse. Just focus on the ones that speak to you. There is room at the end of this chapter to write your thoughts if you wish.

SUGGESTIONS

When you read the Bible, asking these three quick questions can help you apply it to your own life:

- What does this say about God?
- What does this say about people?
- What does this say about me?

When you pray, don't forget to listen! Spend some time in silence with God. You may ask Him to speak to you and let your mind wander to see where He leads you. You may meditate on a Bible verse or a particular question. Practice being still and doing nothing during this time.

Set aside a time of day when you are at your best to spend a few minutes reflecting on your day. Write down your successes, failures, who you need to forgive, and any amends you need to make. Or, you may answer some of the questions below on a daily basis. Writing these things down will come in handy when doing a long-term evaluation in the future.

QUESTIONS

The following questions are designed to help jumpstart your thinking.

- Am I comfortable reading the Bible and understanding it? If not, can I ask a trusted friend or pastor for help?
- What does it mean to me to pray only for God's will and not my own?
- How can I distinguish between God's will and my self-will?
- How can I accept God's will even when it's difficult?
- How has my own will caused me difficulties?
- When life gets tough, what will motivate me to continue examining my stuff?
- How can I give myself grace in this process?

In my daily check I can ask myself:

- What was good today? What was difficult today?
- How did I respond to difficulties or hurts?
- Did I trust God today? Or did I act in fear or arrogance?

- Did I try to manipulate, fix, or control anyone today?
- Do I owe anyone amends for anything that happened today?
- Do I need to forgive someone for something that happened today?
- Is there anything I need to confess to God today? To someone I trust?
- How can I treat myself with patience and grace when I continue to make mistakes?
- Did I do something I really didn't want to do today? Was that growth or lack of trust? What were my motives?
- Did I keep silent in order to avoid conflict when I should have spoken up? What were my motives?
- How was my character today? What situations brought out my positive character traits? What situations brought out my negative character traits?
- Did I say "yes" to something when I should have said "no"?
- Was I able to stand up for myself today? If not, what could help me?
- Did I take on a responsibility that was not mine? What will happen if I don't? How can I trust God with that?
- If I discovered that I was wrong, did I admit it or did I hide it?
- If I'm afraid my mistakes will be used against me, what will give me the courage to admit them anyway?
- Do I have stuff that keeps coming up when I check my direction? Do I agree with God that it is harmful? Why am I holding on to it?

RELATED SCRIPTURE

Look over the following verses. How do they relate to seeking God's will and continuing to examine yourself daily?

Isaiah 55:8-9

I Corinthians 10:12-13

Galatians 2:11-13, 17-18

Ephesians 4:21-32

Ephesians 5:15-16

Philippians 4:8-9

Philippians 4:6-8

James 4:1-10

More verses on this subject:
Joshua 1:8, Psalm 1:1-3, Psalm 13, Psalm 25:4-5, Psalm 119:105-106, Proverbs 15:14, Isaiah 30:18, Matthew 6:6, Matthew 7:7-11, Luke 6:46-49, Philippians 2:3-4, 2 Timothy 3:16-17

Daily Check Journal

What was good today? Where do I see God working in my character? Was I honest today? What was bad today? How did I respond? Am I trusting God? What was my part in the problem? Did I try to control or avoid?

What were my expectations? Were they realistic? Did I give someone grace today? Do I need to give myself grace? Do I owe anyone an amends? Do I need to forgive anyone? What trait or problem is recurring in my daily check?

What was good today? Where do I see God working in my character? Was I honest today? What was bad today? How did I respond? Am I trusting God? What was my part in the problem? Did I try to control or avoid?

What were my expectations? Were they realistic? Did I give someone grace today? Do I need to give myself grace? Do I owe anyone an amends? Do I need to forgive anyone? What trait or problem is recurring in my daily check?

What was good today? Where do I see God working in my character? Was I honest today? What was bad today? How did I respond? Am I trusting God? What was my part in the problem? Did I try to control or avoid?

What were my expectations? Were they realistic? Did I give someone grace today? Do I need to give myself grace? Do I owe anyone an amends? Do I need to forgive anyone? What trait or problem is recurring in my daily check?

What was good today? Where do I see God working in my character? Was I honest today? What was bad today? How did I respond? Am I trusting God? What was my part in the problem? Did I try to control or avoid?

What were my expectations? Were they realistic? Did I give someone grace today? Do I need to give myself grace? Do I owe anyone an amends? Do I need to forgive anyone? What trait or problem is recurring in my daily check?

What was good today? Where do I see God working in my character? Was I honest today? What was bad today? How did I respond? Am I trusting God? What was my part in the problem? Did I try to control or avoid?

What were my expectations? Were they realistic? Did I give someone grace today? Do I need to give myself grace? Do I owe anyone an amends? Do I need to forgive anyone? What trait or problem is recurring in my daily check?

What was good today? Where do I see God working in my character? Was I honest today? What was bad today? How did I respond? Am I trusting God? What was my part in the problem? Did I try to control or avoid?

What were my expectations? Were they realistic? Did I give someone grace today? Do I need to give myself grace?
Do I owe anyone an amends? Do I need to forgive anyone? What trait or problem is recurring in my daily check?

What was good today? Where do I see God working in my character? Was I honest today? What was bad today? How did I respond? Am I trusting God? What was my part in the problem? Did I try to control or avoid?

What were my expectations? Were they realistic? Did I give someone grace today? Do I need to give myself grace? Do I owe anyone an amends? Do I need to forgive anyone? What trait or problem is recurring in my daily check?

What was good today? Where do I see God working in my character? Was I honest today? What was bad today? How did I respond? Am I trusting God? What was my part in the problem? Did I try to control or avoid?

What were my expectations? Were they realistic? Did I give someone grace today? Do I need to give myself grace? Do I owe anyone an amends? Do I need to forgive anyone? What trait or problem is recurring in my daily check?

What was good today? Where do I see God working in my character? Was I honest today? What was bad today? How did I respond? Am I trusting God? What was my part in the problem? Did I try to control or avoid?

What were my expectations? Were they realistic? Did I give someone grace today? Do I need to give myself grace? Do I owe anyone an amends? Do I need to forgive anyone? What trait or problem is recurring in my daily check?

What was good today? Where do I see God working in my character? Was I honest today? What was bad today? How did I respond? Am I trusting God? What was my part in the problem? Did I try to control or avoid?

What were my expectations? Were they realistic? Did I give someone grace today? Do I need to give myself grace? Do I owe anyone an amends? Do I need to forgive anyone? What trait or problem is recurring in my daily check?

What was good today? Where do I see God working in my character? Was I honest today? What was bad today? How did I respond? Am I trusting God? What was my part in the problem? Did I try to control or avoid?

What were my expectations? Were they realistic? Did I give someone grace today? Do I need to give myself grace? Do I owe anyone an amends? Do I need to forgive anyone? What trait or problem is recurring in my daily check?

What was good today? Where do I see God working in my character? Was I honest today? What was bad today? How did I respond? Am I trusting God? What was my part in the problem? Did I try to control or avoid?

What were my expectations? Were they realistic? Did I give someone grace today? Do I need to give myself grace? Do I owe anyone an amends? Do I need to forgive anyone? What trait or problem is recurring in my daily check?

What was good today? Where do I see God working in my character? Was I honest today? What was bad today? How did I respond? Am I trusting God? What was my part in the problem? Did I try to control or avoid?

What were my expectations? Were they realistic? Did I give someone grace today? Do I need to give myself grace? Do I owe anyone an amends? Do I need to forgive anyone? What trait or problem is recurring in my daily check?

What was good today? Where do I see God working in my character? Was I honest today? What was bad today? How did I respond? Am I trusting God? What was my part in the problem? Did I try to control or avoid?

What were my expectations? Were they realistic? Did I give someone grace today? Do I need to give myself grace? Do I owe anyone an amends? Do I need to forgive anyone? What trait or problem is recurring in my daily check?

What was good today? Where do I see God working in my character? Was I honest today? What was bad today? How did I respond? Am I trusting God? What was my part in the problem? Did I try to control or avoid?

What were my expectations? Were they realistic? Did I give someone grace today? Do I need to give myself grace? Do I owe anyone an amends? Do I need to forgive anyone? What trait or problem is recurring in my daily check?

What was good today? Where do I see God working in my character? Was I honest today? What was bad today? How did I respond? Am I trusting God? What was my part in the problem? Did I try to control or avoid?

What were my expectations? Were they realistic? Did I give someone grace today? Do I need to give myself grace? Do I owe anyone an amends? Do I need to forgive anyone? What trait or problem is recurring in my daily check?

What was good today? Where do I see God working in my character? Was I honest today? What was bad today? How did I respond? Am I trusting God? What was my part in the problem? Did I try to control or avoid?

What were my expectations? Were they realistic? Did I give someone grace today? Do I need to give myself grace? Do I owe anyone an amends? Do I need to forgive anyone? What trait or problem is recurring in my daily check?

What was good today? Where do I see God working in my character? Was I honest today? What was bad today? How did I respond? Am I trusting God? What was my part in the problem? Did I try to control or avoid?

What were my expectations? Were they realistic? Did I give someone grace today? Do I need to give myself grace? Do I owe anyone an amends? Do I need to forgive anyone? What trait or problem is recurring in my daily check?

What was good today? Where do I see God working in my character? Was I honest today? What was bad today? How did I respond? Am I trusting God? What was my part in the problem? Did I try to control or avoid?

What were my expectations? Were they realistic? Did I give someone grace today? Do I need to give myself grace? Do I owe anyone an amends? Do I need to forgive anyone? What trait or problem is recurring in my daily check?

What was good today? Where do I see God working in my character? Was I honest today? What was bad today? How did I respond? Am I trusting God? What was my part in the problem? Did I try to control or avoid?

What were my expectations? Were they realistic? Did I give someone grace today? Do I need to give myself grace? Do I owe anyone an amends? Do I need to forgive anyone? What trait or problem is recurring in my daily check?

What was good today? Where do I see God working in my character? Was I honest today? What was bad today? How did I respond? Am I trusting God? What was my part in the problem? Did I try to control or avoid?

What were my expectations? Were they realistic? Did I give someone grace today? Do I need to give myself grace? Do I owe anyone an amends? Do I need to forgive anyone? What trait or problem is recurring in my daily check?

What was good today? Where do I see God working in my character? Was I honest today? What was bad today? How did I respond? Am I trusting God? What was my part in the problem? Did I try to control or avoid?

What were my expectations? Were they realistic? Did I give someone grace today? Do I need to give myself grace? Do I owe anyone an amends? Do I need to forgive anyone? What trait or problem is recurring in my daily check?

What was good today? Where do I see God working in my character? Was I honest today? What was bad today? How did I respond? Am I trusting God? What was my part in the problem? Did I try to control or avoid?

What were my expectations? Were they realistic? Did I give someone grace today? Do I need to give myself grace? Do I owe anyone an amends? Do I need to forgive anyone? What trait or problem is recurring in my daily check?

What was good today? Where do I see God working in my character? Was I honest today? What was bad today? How did I respond? Am I trusting God? What was my part in the problem? Did I try to control or avoid?

What were my expectations? Were they realistic? Did I give someone grace today? Do I need to give myself grace?
Do I owe anyone an amends? Do I need to forgive anyone? What trait or problem is recurring in my daily check?

What was good today? Where do I see God working in my character? Was I honest today? What was bad today? How did I respond? Am I trusting God? What was my part in the problem? Did I try to control or avoid?

What were my expectations? Were they realistic? Did I give someone grace today? Do I need to give myself grace? Do I owe anyone an amends? Do I need to forgive anyone? What trait or problem is recurring in my daily check?

What was good today? Where do I see God working in my character? Was I honest today? What was bad today? How did I respond? Am I trusting God? What was my part in the problem? Did I try to control or avoid?

What were my expectations? Were they realistic? Did I give someone grace today? Do I need to give myself grace? Do I owe anyone an amends? Do I need to forgive anyone? What trait or problem is recurring in my daily check?

What was good today? Where do I see God working in my character? Was I honest today? What was bad today? How did I respond? Am I trusting God? What was my part in the problem? Did I try to control or avoid?

What were my expectations? Were they realistic? Did I give someone grace today? Do I need to give myself grace? Do I owe anyone an amends? Do I need to forgive anyone? What trait or problem is recurring in my daily check?

The Path

Group Leader's Guide

STARTING A GROUP

Let me start off by saying that the group leader's role is that of a facilitator, not a teacher. As the leader, your job is to make sure the meeting runs smoothly using the guidelines below, but you are not responsible for correcting others, providing answers to problems, making people share, or making sure people come to your group. You are simply there to facilitate the group, and participate yourself. Hopefully you will encourage others to facilitate after the group has been meeting for a while.

Ideally, small groups will be offered continually so that they are always available to those who need them. It can take years for an individual to personally work through the whole process. Since sharing is such an important part of that, having a group available is important. I realize that having a continual group may not work in every situation. Another option is to provide this study once a year. We need the repetition of going over these principles again and again before they truly sink in. If you continue to provide these groups it brings about an interesting dynamic. While the group will be studying the same chapter in the meeting, each individual may be at a different point in the process. For example, it may take one person six months to get to the point of completing an examination of their stuff, while it may take another person two years to complete. Whatever stage each person is working through, everyone will be able to contribute to, and get something out of, the meeting.

It is imperative that this type of small group has an atmosphere of safety and openness. We must feel free to share our thoughts and discoveries without judgment or advice. If a group does not promote this kind of atmosphere, the group will die.

Ideally, it is recommended that you have a women's group and a men's group. Women have issues that should only be shared with women and the same goes for men. Spouses must feel free to share struggles in their marriage without embarrassing one another, or share their feelings about other issues that they know their spouse disagrees with. If you don't have enough people to have separate groups don't let that stop you! Go ahead and have a combined group. The women and men can talk about difficult issues at a different time. Or you could separate once a month and ask if anyone needs to share something that couldn't be shared in a mixed group. You could also have a group that meets together for the reading and then splits for discussion. Depth and honesty in personal sharing is so important to our growth; facilitate it in any way you can.

GROUP STRUCTURE

The following is the suggested structure of the meeting and the guidelines that a group must follow in order to provide a smooth meeting and promote trust and freedom in sharing our experiences.

Pray
Read the Group Guidelines (see the explanations below)
Read the chapter out loud, pausing to answer the group discussion questions.

> Reading the study at the meeting makes it as easy as possible for everyone to participate. Go around the room and have each person read a paragraph. Of course, a person can pass if they choose to.

Share your thoughts at the end of the chapter.

> I recommend going around the room, it helps everyone feel that they can speak up and it keeps others from continually butting in. People can share life experiences, thoughts on the chapter, responses to the questions, problems and discouragement, discoveries and growth. They may share how they handled a problem brought up by someone else as long as it doesn't turn into advice ("I found" vs. "you should"). Remember the Guidelines.

> One note of caution, some members may share information which is too detailed, graphic, or personal. For example, details of abuse, sexual issues, or something that embarrasses someone else. If this happens, talk to that person in private after the meeting. Thank them for being vulnerable to the group and tell the person that the information they are sharing is too much detail for the group setting, but would be the perfect thing to share with a trusted friend.

Read the **LOCATION CHECK** suggestions and questions
Share your thoughts
Read Scripture
Share your thoughts
Pray

The above is a suggestion; you can tailor it to your own group. You could read through everything before opening it up to sharing and then go through the verses. You could let people read the **LOCATION CHECK** section on their own and just skip to the verses. What works best will depend on you and the people in your group. Be flexible.

Make sure you, as the facilitator, hang around until everyone has left in case someone needs to talk or ask a question. You won't have all the answers, but you can listen and pray with someone. You can relate your experiences. Or, you can acknowledge the difficulty of their struggles and encourage them to keep coming back. Help and fellowship is here, if we will take it.

GROUP GUIDELINES

These guidelines are on page 6 and should be read at the start of each meeting to remind people of their responsibility as part of this group. As a group facilitator, you will be responsible for making sure the members of the group follow the guidelines and don't start giving advice, judging, or taking over the discussion. Here is an explanation of each of the Group Guidelines and some helpful tips for keeping people on track.

> Focus on your own thoughts and behavior, not on blaming others or on what other people have shared.

If we are not careful, meetings can turn into pity parties or spouse bashing sessions. The purpose of this group is to examine our own motives and actions. While it may be of some benefit to mention our struggle with someone or something (sometimes we must vent before we can think), we must focus on our behavior, thoughts, response, or reaction to that situation. If we do not look at ourselves, we will gain nothing but bitterness.

Here are a few questions and statements to pull a member back from blaming. "How has that affected your behavior?" "What does this situation say about you?" "Let's try to think about our behavior as we share." "Remember, this meeting is about us, not others."

> Do not give advice to anyone or correct anything anyone shares. It doesn't matter if they're way off in your theological opinion, they need to share freely in order to figure out their own stuff. Let them. If you're unsure about the scriptural truth of something shared, look it up yourself or ask your pastor.

Romans 14:4 says, "Who are you to condemn God's servants? They are responsible to the Lord, so let Him tell them whether they are right or wrong. The Lord's power will help them do as they should." Right or wrong, we all need to feel free to share what is in our hearts and minds without judgment of any kind. Each of us is different and the Holy Spirit is working differently in each of our lives. None of us knows what is best for someone else. When we feel free to share anything, even if we haven't quite figured things out yet, we make ourselves open to hearing God and discovering His will.

Conversely, if we get advice from others when we share it makes us less open. We feel stupid for wrestling with our particular issues or we resent the advice giver who has not walked in our shoes. As a result we close ourselves to hearing God through others and may ignore the very solution that could work for us. We must give others the dignity of finding their own solutions and coming to their own conclusions.

If you need to stop someone from giving advice you could say, "Remember, we're not giving advice, we're dealing with our own issues." Or, "Make sure you're not telling him what to do, talk about your own experience in that area." Or you could say, "Can you continue using 'I' statements instead of 'you' statements?" After the meeting, you could repeat the last sentence of this guideline to remind people to seek additional godly council regarding anything that has been said.

> Don't interrupt anyone; let them finish their thoughts, even if they're stumbling
> through them.

We all should be treated with respect. This is not the sort of group where we build on what others have said with conversation bouncing around the room like a runaway racquetball. We are allowed to share until we are finished (within reason) no matter how disjointed or hesitant we sound. Some of us come to conclusions by talking things out, and to be interrupted disrupts the process.

You can say things like, "Please wait until she's finished." "One at a time, please." Or, you may wait until the interrupter is finished and then ask the other person, "Were you finished sharing or would you like to continue?" If you have read the Group Guidelines at the start of the meeting, the interrupter should get the point.

> Don't talk with your neighbor while someone is sharing.

This is pretty self-explanatory. Basically, you do not want two or three people talking about something while the rest of the group is waiting patiently for their turn to share. Or, worse yet, we do not want a separate conversation going on while others are trying to share.

You can interject with statements like these. "Oops, let's all listen to what _____ has to say." Or, "Why don't we continue discussing that after the meeting? Let's continue with sharing." Or, "Let's not talk while someone else is sharing."

> Don't hog sharing time; keep it to a few minutes so that everyone has a chance.

This guideline allows everyone to have a chance to share. Many times people want to focus on their particular issue, but aren't interested in listening to anyone else. Or, they just like hearing themselves talk. The group time is not a time to come and dump at the expense of the group. You might encourage someone to hang around and talk after the meetings if they need to share more or talk one on one. Some people are just story-tellers that lose track of time. A simple reminder is all that is necessary to help them wrap up.

Simply saying, "It's time to finish your thought," is sufficient. You could also say, "Thank you for sharing. Let's have _____ share next." Or, "We may have time for you to share more on that later." If your group is under ten people, you should have plenty of time for everyone to share a few times.

Above all else, do not talk about what anyone shares outside of this group. Respecting confidentiality is essential for honesty. If you break confidence you may be asked to leave the group because it will be harder for people to be open and honest around you.

Again, members must feel free to share what is in their hearts and minds without fear of being talked about. Even members in the same group must NOT talk about what someone else has shared in the meeting. We have enough to do just handling our own lives without getting into the business of discussing others. James 5:16 says, "Confess your sins to each other and pray for each other so that you may be healed." If we must confess our sins to each other, we should be able to trust those to whom we share.

If you find out that something was shared outside the group you should have a conversation with that person and the one talked about. Give the "talker" a chance to make amends. It could be resolved easily or it could be a significant breach of trust that will be difficult to reestablish which will stifle vital sharing. If it's significant enough to affect the group's openness you should ask that person not to come back. You may decide to tell the group that the person was asked to leave because confidentiality was breached. Or, you may decide to just tell the person who was offended. You may want to discuss the options with a trusted friend before you act as every situation is unique. You will have to evaluate whether or not you will let someone who has broken confidence into another group.

It may take a while for everyone to catch on to the unique atmosphere of the meeting. Most will respond positively to your reminders – especially if you have read the Group Guidelines at the start of the meeting. Once the atmosphere is established, new members will catch on quickly.

NOTES:

1   Benson, C. Irving. The Eight Points of the Oxford Group. Melbourne: Humphrey Milford Oxford University Press, 1938. p.7

2   Anderson, Neil. Victory over the Darkness. Ventura: Regal Books, 1990. p.45

3   Anderson, Neil. Victory over the Darkness. Ventura: Regal Books, 1990. pp.45-47

4   Al-Anon Family Groups. Paths to Recovery. Virginia Beach: Al-Anon, 1997. p.41

5   Benson, C. Irving. The Eight Points of the Oxford Group. Melbourne: Humphrey Milford Oxford University Press, 1938. p.36

6   Benson, C. Irving. The Eight Points of the Oxford Group. Melbourne: Humphrey Milford Oxford University Press, 1938. p.107

7   Warren, Rick. The Purpose Driven Life. Michigan: Zondervan, 2002. p.275

Printed in the United States
By Bookmasters